Cisco ENCOR
350-401
Exam Questions and Answers dumps

(New Edition 2020)

No Answers Spoiling
-Answers are found at the end of the book-

Implementing Cisco Enterprise Network Core Technologies

By EXAM BOOST

The information contained in the book is provided for educational and informational purposes only

Pass Cisco ENCOR 350-401 Exam in First Attempt Guaranteed.

This book contains Real Exam Questions, Accurate & Verified Answers As Seen in the Real Exam.

Vendor: Cisco
Certifications: CCNP Enterprise
Exam Name: Implementing and Operating Cisco Enterprise Network Core Technologies (ENCOR)
Exam Code: 350-401 ENCOR
Total Questions: 60 Questions and Answers

These questions test your knowledge and skills related to implementing core enterprise network technologies, including:

- Dual stack (IPv4 and IPv6) architecture
- Virtualization
- Infrastructure
- Network assurance
- Security
- Automation

No Answers Spoiling! You will find the answers in a table at the end of the book.

QUESTION 1

You issue the ping 192.168.1.1 size 1600 command on a Cisco device that is configured with the default system MTU. All pings succeed. Which of the following is most likely true? (Select the best answer.)

A.   The interface is configured with an MTU of at least 1,600.
• B.   The pings were sent to the destination in a fragmented fashion.
C.   The DF bit has been enabled, causing the pings to succeed.
D.   The datagram size specified is below the default MTU value.

Correct Answer: (Look at the end of the book)

Explanation/Reference:
Explanation:

Most likely, the pings were sent to the destination in a fragmented fashion because the IP version 4 (IPv4) donotfragment bit, or DF bit, has not been set in this scenario. By default, packet fragmentation is used to enable oversized packets to traverse the network in chunks that are smaller than the configured maximum transmission unit (MTU.) Enabling the DF bit configures the ping command to attempt to send packets of a given size without fragmentation. By repeatedly pinging a destination device with smaller and smaller datagram sizes, you can determine the MTU.

The ping command supports the ability to modify the size of the datagram that it transmits as well as the ability to enable the DF bit, which is disabled by default. You can configure extended ping features either by issuing the ping command without parameters, which causes the ping command to display a series of configuration prompts, or by specifying parameters on the command line along with the ping command. For example, the ping 192.168.1.1 size 1500 dfbit command configures an extended ping with a destination IP address of 192.168.1.1, a datagram size of 1,500 bytes, and an enabled DF bit. On a connection with an MTU of 1,500 bytes, this ping succeeds, as shown in the following output:

```
RouterA#ping 192.168.1.1 size 1500 df-bit
Type escape sequence to abort.
Sending 5, 1500-byte ICMP Echos to 192.168.1.1, timeout is 2 seconds:
Packet sent with the DF bit set
!!!!!
Success rate is 100 percent (5/5), round-trip min/avg/max = 16/20/36 m
```

Based on the output, you can determine that the ping succeeded. You can also determine that the DF bit is, indeed, enabled. However, issuing the ping 192.168.1.1 size 1501 dfbit command on the same device results in a failure, as shown in the following output:

```
RouterA#ping 192.168.1.1 size 1501 df-bit
Type escape sequence to abort.
Sending 5, 1501-byte ICMP Echos to 192.168.1.1, timeout is 2 seconds:
Packet sent with the DF bit set
.....
Success rate is 0 percent (0/5)
```

In the output above, issuing the ping 192.168.1.1 size 1501 dfbit command results in a ping failure because the MTU is configured to 1,500 bytes and the DF bit is set. If you were to issue the same command without the dfbit parameter, the ping would succeed because the ping command is allowing the datagram to be fragmented, as shown in the following output:

```
RouterA#ping 192.168.1.1 size 1501
Type escape sequence to abort.
Sending 5, 1501-byte ICMP Echos to 192.168.1.1, timeout is 2 seconds:
!!!!!
Success rate is 100 percent (5/5), round-trip min/avg/max = 16/19/20 m
```

The interface is not configured with an MTU value of at least 1,600 in this scenario. In addition, the datagram size specified is not below the default MTU value on a Cisco device. By default, a Cisco device has a system MTU of 1,500 bytes. In this scenario, you have issued the ping 192.168.1.1 size 1600 command on a device that is configured with the system default MTU.

The DF bit has not been enabled in this scenario. In order to enable the DF bit, you should issue the ping command with the dfbit parameter. Reference:

Cisco: Using the Extended ping and Extended traceroute

Commands: The Extended ping Command

QUESTION 2

You administer the network in the following exhibit:

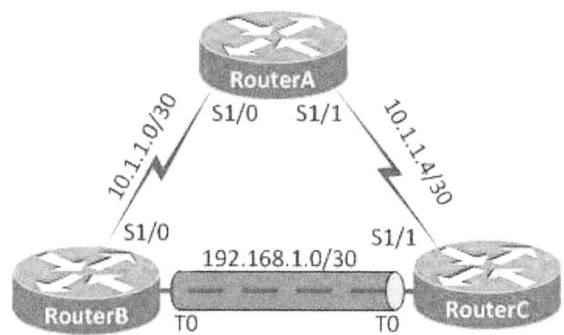

All routers are configured to the system MTU defaults.
You issue the ping 192.168.1.2 size 1500 dfbit command from
RouterB, but the ping fails. Which of the following is most likely the
cause of the failure? (Select the best answer.)

- A.   The GRE tunnel MTU is 1,476.
  B.   The system default MTU is 1,400.

  C.   The DF bit is not enabled.
  D.   The GRE tunnel does not support fragmented datagrams.

Correct Answer: (Look at the end of the book)

Explanation/Reference:
Explanation:

Most likely, the Generic Routing Encapsulation (GRE) tunnel
maximum transmission unit (MTU) is 1,476 if the ping fails in this
scenario. By default, Cisco routers are configured with a system MTU
of 1,500 bytes, which includes a 20byte IP header and 1,480 bytes of
payload. The ping 192.168.1.2 size 1500 dfbit command in this
scenario attempts to send a datagram of 1,500 bytes to a destination

address of 192.168.1.2 without fragmenting the datagram into smaller pieces.

In this scenario, the donotfragment, or DF bit, has been enabled with the pingcommand. When the DF bit is set, the device attempts to send packets without fragmentation. If the packet is larger than the MTU, the attempt will fail. Because the GRE tunnel's MTU supports a maximum of 1,476 bytes, a ping with a size of 1,500 bytes that does not permit fragmentation will fail.

GRE tunnels add a 24byte header to an IP packet. However, a default GRE tunnel MTU is 24 bytes smaller than the MTU of the physical interface. When the DF bit is not set, an unencapsulated 1,500byte packet would be split into two unencapsulated packets: a 1,476byte packet and a 44byte packet, prior to being transported across the tunnel. This process enables each fragment of the packet to include the 24byte GRE header when it traverses the physical interface that is being used as the tunnel's source. The total sizes of the packet fragments that traverse the physical interface thus become 1,500 bytes and 68 bytes, respectively.

The DF bit is enabled in this scenario. The ping command supports the ability to modify the size of the datagram it transmits as well as the ability to enable the DF bit, which is disabled by default. You can configure extended ping features either by issuing the pingcommand without parameters, which causes the ping command to display a series of configuration prompts, or by specifying parameters on the command line along with the ping command. For example, the ping 192.168.1.1 size 1500 dfbit command configures an extended ping with a destination IP address of 192.168.1.1, a datagram size of 1,500 bytes, and an enabled DF bit.

The system default MTU on Cisco devices is 1,500, not 1,400. Therefore, a system default MTU of 1,400 is not causing the failure in this scenario. In addition, GRE tunnels do support fragmented datagrams.

Reference:
Cisco: Resolve IP Fragmentation, MTU, MSS, and PMTUD Issues

with GRE and IPSEC: Scenario 5

QUESTION 3

Which of the following is not a GRE tunnel state on a Cisco device? (Select the best answer.)

A. Administratively down/down
B. Down/up
C. Reset/down
D. Up/down
E. Up/up

Correct Answer: (Look at the end of the book)

Explanation/Reference:
Explanation:

Down/up is not a Generic Routing Encapsulation (GRE) tunnel state on a Cisco device. Nor is Down/up a valid state for any other connection on a Cisco device, because a line protocol cannot be in the up state when an interface is in the Down or Administratively down state. Interface states and line protocol states are often presented as a single connection state separated by a slash. The state preceding the slash represents the interface state. The state succeeding the slash represents the line protocol state. In order for the line protocol state to be up, the interface state must also be up.

A GRE tunnel can exist in one of the following four states:
-    Administratively down/down
-    Reset/down
-    Up/down
-    Up/up

A tunnel in the Administratively down/down state has been configured with the shutdown command. By default, a tunnel interface automatically transitions to the upstate when it is created. Therefore, it is not normally necessary to issue the no shutdowncommand to bring a tunnel interface up unless you have previously issued the shutdowncommand.

A tunnel in the Reset/down state is typically transiting through that state because a software interface reset has occurred. Software resets can happen if the tunnel is misconfigured. For example, a software reset might occur if a tunnel interface has been configured to use its own IP address as a next hop.

A tunnel in the Up/down state indicates that the tunnel interface is configured but something is interfering with the line protocol. This state commonly occurs when the tunnel interface is configured to use an incorrect destination address or when the physical interface has no route to the tunnel's destination address. It can also occur if the tunnel destination address lies through the tunnel itself.

A tunnel in the Up/up state indicates that both the tunnel interface and the line protocol are up and functional. If something is preventing communication between endpoints on opposite ends of the tunnel and the tunnel is in the Up/up state on each end, you should continue troubleshooting beyond the tunnel configuration.

Reference:
Cisco: GRE Tunnel Interface States and What Impacts Them: Four Different Tunnel States

QUESTION 4

Which of the following ping command options should be enabled if you want to determine the MTU size that a given connection supports? (Select the best answer.)

A.   the IPv4 donotfragment bit
B.   a number of pings greater than five
C.   a datagram size greater than 1,500 bytes
D.   a timeout value greater than two seconds

Correct Answer: (Look at the end of the book)

Explanation/Reference:

Explanation:

The IP version 4 (IPv4) donotfragment bit, or DF bit, is the ping command option that should be enabled if you want to determine the maximum transmission unit (MTU) size that a given connection supports. By default, packet fragmentation is used to enable oversized packets to traverse the network in chunks that are smaller than the configured MTU. The DF bit configures the ping command to attempt to send packets of a given size without fragmentation. By repeatedly pinging a destination device with smaller and smaller datagram sizes, you can determine the MTU.

The ping command supports the ability to modify the size of the datagram that it transmits as well as the ability to enable the DF bit, which is disabled by default. You can configure extended ping features either by issuing the ping command without parameters, which causes the ping command to display a series of configuration prompts, or by specifying parameters on the command line along with the ping command. For example, the ping 192.168.1.1 size 1500 dfbit command configures an extended ping with a destination IP address of 192.168.1.1, a datagram size of 1,500 bytes, and an enabled DF bit. On a connection with an MTU of 1,500 bytes, this ping succeeds, as shown in the following output:

```
RouterA#ping 192.168.1.1 size 1500 df-bit
Type escape sequence to abort.
Sending 5, 1500-byte ICMP Echos to 192.168.1.1, timeout is 2 seconds:
Packet sent with the DF bit set
!!!!!
Success rate is 100 percent (5/5), round-trip min/avg/max = 16/20/36 m
```

Based on the output, you can determine that the ping succeeded. You can also determine that the DF bit is, indeed, enabled. However, issuing the ping 192.168.1.1 size 1501 dfbit command on the same device results in a failure, as shown in the following output:

```
RouterA#ping 192.168.1.1 size 1501 df-bit
Type escape sequence to abort.
Sending 5, 1501-byte ICMP Echos to 192.168.1.1, timeout is 2 seconds:
Packet sent with the DF bit set
.....
Success rate is 0 percent (0/5)
```

In the output above, issuing the ping 192.168.1.1 size 1501 dfbit command results in a ping failure because the MTU is configured to 1,500 bytes and the DF bit is set. If you were to issue the same command without the dfbit parameter, the ping would succeed because the ping command is allowing the datagram to be fragmented, as shown in the following output:

```
RouterA#ping 192.168.1.1 size 1501
Type escape sequence to abort.
Sending 5, 1501-byte ICMP Echos to 192.168.1.1, timeout is 2 seconds:
!!!!!
Success rate is 100 percent (5/5), round-trip min/avg/max = 16/19/20 m
```

You do not need to explicitly set the datagram size to 1,500 bytes in this scenario. By default, Cisco devices are configured with a system MTU of 1,500 bytes. Therefore, the ping might succeed, providing no indication of a configured MTU. In order to test the MTU, you should set the DF bit and test a high MTU. You should then methodically lower the datagram size that you test with the DF bit enabled until the ping succeeds.

You do not need to adjust the number of pings from the default value of five. In addition, you do not need to adjust the default timeout value of two seconds. Neither of these values help you determine the configured MTU.

Reference:
Cisco: Using the Extended ping and Extended traceroute Commands: The Extended ping Command

QUESTION 5

You issue the debug ppp authentication command on RouterA. RouterA's Serial 0/0 interface is connected to RouterB. RouterA's Serial 0/1 interface is connected to RouterC. You issue the no shutdown command on all interfaces and note that every interface has entered the up state.

Next, you issue the show debug condition command on RouterA and receive the following output:

```
Condition 1: interface Se0/0 (0 flags triggered)
        Flags: Se0/0
Condition 2: interface Se0/1 (1 flags triggered)
        Flags: Se0/1
Condition 3: username RouterB (0 flags triggered)
```

Which of the following statements is true? (Select the best answer.)

A.   A debug condition has been met on the Serial 0/0 interface.
◄ B.   A debug condition has been met on the Serial 0/1 interface.
C.   A debug condition has been met in which the user name is RouterB.
D.   All debug conditions in this scenario have been met.
E.   None of the debug conditions in this scenario have been met.

Correct Answer: (Look at the end of the book)

Explanation/Reference:
Explanation:

Based on the output in this scenario, you can determine that a PointtoPoint Protocol (PPP) authentication debug condition has been met on the Serial 0/1 interface of RouterA, which is the interface that is connected to RouterC. The debug condition command is used to enable restrictions on the data that the debugging process displays. If no conditions are specified, all output from enabled debugging commands will be displayed. You can configure a series of debug conditions, any one of which will cause debug messages to display when a match occurs. In order to display the output, the debugging process need only match one of the specified conditions, not all of them.

You can determine which debug conditions are configured and which have been met on a Cisco device by issuing the show debug condition command from privileged EXEC mode. For example, the following output indicates that three conditions have been enabled on the router, but only one condition has been matched so far:

```
RouterA#show debug condition
Condition 1: interface Se0/0 (0 flags triggered)
        Flags: Se0/0
Condition 2: interface Se0/1 (1 flags triggered)
        Flags: Se0/1
Condition 3: username RouterB (0 flags triggered)
```

Because you have enabled PPP authentication debugging in this scenario, you can determine that PPP authentication has occurred on RouterA's Serial 0/1 interface. In addition, you can determine that the user name RouterB has not been triggered. Therefore, no PPP authentication has occurred on RouterA that includes the user name of RouterB.

The debug condition interfaceinterface command limits debug messaging output to only enabled debugging that applies to the specified interface. For example, if you were to issue the debug condition interface serial 0/0 command followed by the debug ppp authentication command in this scenario, the debug output would consist of PPP authentication messages, but only if those messages also apply to the router's Serial 0/0 interface.

Configuring a series of debug condition interface interface commands limits debug message output to the series of specified interfaces. The debug output need match only one of the interface conditions to be displayed. For example, you could issue the following commands on RouterA to ensure that PPP authentication debug messages that apply to either the Serial 0/0 interface or the Serial 0/1 interface are displayed on the router:

```
RouterA#debug condition interface serial 0/0
RouterA#debug condition interface serial 0/1
RouterA#debug ppp authentication
```

After issuing the commands above, you could further limit the PPP authentication debug output by issuing the no debug condition interface interface command. For example, issuing the no debug condition interface serial 0/0 command would remove the Serial 0/0 interface condition from the debugging output, which means that only PPP authentication messages that apply to the Serial 0/1 interface would be displayed. You can remove all interface conditions from debugging output by issuing the no debug condition interface all command. After that command is issued, all PPP authentication debugging messages would be displayed unless you also issued the no debug ppp authenticationcommand or the no debug all command.

The debug condition {username username | called dialstring | callerdialstring} command enables you to limit the output of debugging messages by user name, calling party number, or called party number. Applying only one of those conditions to debugging output stops the output of debug messages on all interfaces. The router will then monitor each interface for a condition match. If a match occurs, debug messages will be displayed for that match. In this scenario, the debug condition username RouterB command will display output when an interface sends or receives a PPP authentication packet that contains the user name RouterB. However, because you have also issued the debug condition interface serial 0/0 command and the debug condition interface serial 0/1 command, PPP authentication messages that apply to either of those interfaces will be displayed even if the RouterB user name is not matched.

Reference:
Cisco: Cisco IOS Debug Command Reference, Release 12.2:
Enabling Conditional Debugging Commands

QUESTION 6

You issue the ping 192.168.1.1 size 1501 dfbit command on a Cisco device. You notice a message indicating that the DF bit has been set. However, the ping fails. You want to determine the largest datagram that the connection supports without fragmentation.
Which of the following should you do next? (Select the best answer.)

A.   Issue the command without the dfbit parameter.
B.   Issue the command without the size parameter.
• C.   Issue the command with a lower size parameter value.
D.   Issue the command without the size parameter and without the dfbit parameter.

Correct Answer: (Look at the end of the book)

Explanation/Reference:
Explanation:

You should issue the command with a lower size parameter value to determine the largest datagram that the connection supports without fragmentation. The IP version 4 (IPv4) donotfragment bit, or DF bit, should be enabled if you want to determine the maximum transmission unit (MTU) size that a given connection supports. By default, packet fragmentation is used to enable oversized packets to traverse the network in chunks that are smaller than the configured MTU. The DF bit configures the ping command to attempt to send packets of a given size without fragmentation. By repeatedly pinging a destination device with smaller and smaller datagram sizes, you can determine the MTU.

The ping command supports the ability to modify the size of the datagram that it transmits as well as the ability to enable the DF bit, which is disabled by default. You can configure extended ping features either by issuing the ping command without parameters, which causes the ping command to display a series of configuration prompts, or by specifying parameters on the command line along with the ping command. For example, the ping 192.168.1.1 size 1500 dfbit command configures an extended ping with a destination IP address of 192.168.1.1, a datagram size of 1,500 bytes, and an enabled DF bit. On a connection with an MTU of 1,500 bytes, this ping succeeds, as shown in the following output:

```
RouterA#ping 192.168.1.1 size 1500 df-bit
Type escape sequence to abort.
Sending 5, 1500-byte ICMP Echos to 192.168.1.1, timeout is 2 seconds:
Packet sent with the DF bit set
!!!!!
Success rate is 100 percent (5/5), round-trip min/avg/max = 16/20/36 m
```

Based on the output, you can determine that the ping succeeded. You can also determine that the DF bit is, indeed, enabled. However, issuing the ping 192.168.1.1 size 1501 dfbit command on the same device results in a failure, as shown in the following output:

```
RouterA#ping 192.168.1.1 size 1501 df-bit
Type escape sequence to abort.
Sending 5, 1501-byte ICMP Echos to 192.168.1.1, timeout is 2 seconds:
Packet sent with the DF bit set
.....
Success rate is 0 percent (0/5)
```

In the output above, issuing the ping 192.168.1.1 size 1501 dfbit command results in a ping failure because the MTU is configured to 1,500 bytes and the DF bit is set. If you were to issue the same command without the dfbit parameter, the ping would succeed because the ping command is allowing the datagram to be fragmented, as shown in the following output:

```
RouterA#ping 192.168.1.1 size 1501
Type escape sequence to abort.
Sending 5, 1501-byte ICMP Echos to 192.168.1.1, timeout is 2 seconds:
!!!!!
Success rate is 100 percent (5/5), round-trip min/avg/max = 16/19/20 m
```

You should not issue the command without the dfbit option, because this disables the DF bit and enables datagram fragmentation. Ping attempts with fragmentation enabled will succeed even if the size parameter remains larger than the configured MTU.

You should not issue the command without the size parameter. The size parameter in addition to the presence of the DF bit is what enables you to test which datagrams are larger than the MTU. Without the size parameter, the ping datagram will use its small default size of 100 bytes.

Reference:
Cisco: Using the Extended ping and Extended traceroute Commands: The Extended ping Command

QUESTION 7

Which of the following statements is true regarding OSPF connections over a GRE tunnel? (Select the best answer.)

A.   Traffic is encapsulated and decapsulated by tunnel endpoints.

14

B.   Tunnel headers do not create any additional overhead.
C.   The transit area cannot be a stub area.
D.   Only routing updates are tunneled.

Correct Answer: (Look at the end of the book)

Explanation/Reference:
Explanation:

Traffic is encapsulated and decapsulated by tunnel endpoints when Open Shortest Path First (OSPF) connections are formed over a Generic Routing Encapsulation (GRE) tunnel. All areas in an OSPF internetwork must be directly connected to the backbone area, Area 0. When a direct connection to the backbone area is not possible, a GRE tunnel or a virtual link can be created between two area border routers (ABRs) to connect the remote area to the backbone area through a transit area.

However, there are some important differences between the two methods. Unlike virtual links, a GRE tunnel encapsulates and decapsulates all traffic at the tunnel endpoints, including the routing updates. GRE tunnels can also transit a stub area. However, GRE tunnels create additional headers, adding overhead to the traffic. It is important to note that an adjacency can only remain stable over a GRE tunnel if the destination remains reachable through the tunnel. If the OSPF neighbor is not reachable through the tunnel, OSPF will drop the adjacency.

Only routing updates are tunneled when an OSPF connection is formed over a virtual link. All other traffic is sent natively over the physical links. The following restrictions apply to virtual links:

-       The routers at each end of the virtual link must share a common area.
-       The transit area cannot be a stub area.
-       One of the routers at either end of the virtual link must connect to the backbone area.

It is important to note that adjacencies formed over virtual links are not visible in the output of the show ip ospf neighbors command. In order to verify that an OSPF adjacency has formed over a virtual link, you can examine the output of the show ip ospf virtuallinks command.

Reference:
Cisco: OSPF Virtual Link: Using a GRE Tunnel Instead of a Virtual Link

QUESTION 8

Which of the following does not cause a GRE tunnel endpoint on a Cisco device to enter the Up/down state? (Select the best answer.)

A.   There is no route to the tunnel destination address.
B.   No IP address has been configured on the tunnel interface.
C.   The tunnel destination address lies through the tunnel itself.
D.   The tunnel source is a loopback interface.

Correct Answer: D

Explanation/Reference:
Explanation:

A tunnel source that is a loopback interface will not cause a Generic Routing Encapsulation (GRE) tunnel endpoint on a Cisco device to enter the Up/down state. GRE tunnel interfaces support loopback interfaces as source addresses and IP addresses on loopback interfaces as destination addresses, as long as the destination address is reachable by the source device. Interface states and line protocol states are often presented as a single connection state separated by a slash. The state preceding the slash represents the interface state. The state succeeding the slash represents the line protocol state. In order for the line protocol state to be up, the interface state must also be up.

A GRE tunnel can exist in one of the following four states:
-       Administratively down/down
-       Reset/down

- Up/down
- Up/up

A tunnel in the Administratively down/down state has been configured with the shutdown command. By default, a tunnel interface automatically transitions to the upstate when it is created. Therefore, it is not normally necessary to issue the no shutdowncommand to bring a tunnel interface up unless you have previously issued the shutdown command.

A tunnel in the Reset/down state is typically transiting through that state because a software interface reset has occurred. Software resets can happen if the tunnel is misconfigured. For example, a software reset might occur if a tunnel interface has been configured to use its own IP address as a next hop.

A tunnel in the Up/down state indicates that the tunnel interface is configured but something is interfering with the line protocol. This state commonly occurs when the tunnel interface is configured to use an incorrect destination address or when the physical interface has no route to the tunnel's destination address. It can also occur if the tunnel destination address lies through the tunnel itself.

A tunnel in the Up/up state indicates that both the tunnel interface and the line protocol are up and functional. If something is preventing communication between endpoints on opposite ends of the tunnel and the tunnel is in the Up/up state on each end, you should continue troubleshooting beyond the tunnel configuration.

Reference:
Cisco: GRE Tunnel Interface States and What Impacts Them: Four Different Tunnel States

QUESTION 9

Which of the following cannot be used to connect an OSPF nonbackbone area to the backbone area? (Select the best answer.)

A.   a GRE tunnel that connects to the OSPF backbone area

B.   a virtual link that connects to the OSPF backbone area
C.   a configuration that redistributes the two OSPF areas into another protocol
D.   a direct connection to the OSPF backbone area

Correct Answer: (Look at the end of the book)

Explanation/Reference:
Explanation:

A configuration that redistributes the two Open Shortest Path First (OSPF) areas into another protocol cannot be used to connect an OSPF nonbackbone area to the backbone area. Redistribution can be used to enable devices in two separate autonomous systems (ASes) to connect and communicate. Therefore, you could enable communication between two separate OSPF configurations by redistributing traffic into another protocol that bridges the two ASes. However, you cannot use redistribution to enable an OSPF connection between a nonbackbone area and a backbone area in a single AS.

You can use a direct connection to the OSPF backbone area to connect an OSPF nonbackbone area to the backbone area. All areas in an OSPF internetwork must be directly connected to the backbone area, Area 0. When a direct connection to the backbone area is not possible, either a virtual link or a Generic Routing Encapsulation (GRE) tunnel must be created between two area border routers (ABRs) to connect the remote area to the backbone area through a transit area.
Although it is possible to use either a virtual link or a GRE tunnel to accomplish this task, there are some important differences between the two methods.

Traffic is encapsulated and decapsulated by tunnel endpoints when OSPF connections are formed over a GRE tunnel. All areas in an OSPF internetwork must be directly connected to the backbone area, Area 0. When a direct connection to the backbone area is not possible, a GRE tunnel or a virtual link can be created between two ABRs to connect the remote area to the backbone area through a transit area.

You can use a virtual link that connects to the backbone area. However, only routing updates are tunneled when an OSPF connection is formed over a virtual link. All other traffic is sent natively over the physical links. The following restrictions apply to virtual links:

-       The routers at each end of the virtual link must share a common area.
-       The transit area cannot be a stub area.
-       One of the routers at either end of the virtual link must connect to the backbone area.

It is important to note that adjacencies formed over virtual links are not visible in the output of the show ip ospf neighbors command. In order to verify that an OSPF adjacency has formed over a virtual link, you can examine the output of the show ip ospf virtuallinks command.

You can use a GRE tunnel that connects to the backbone area. Unlike virtual links, a GRE tunnel encapsulates and decapsulates all traffic at the tunnel endpoints, including the routing updates. GRE tunnels can also transit a stub area. However, GRE tunnels create additional headers, adding overhead to the traffic. It is important to note that an adjacency can only remain stable over a GRE tunnel if the destination remains reachable through the tunnel. If the OSPF neighbor is not reachable through the tunnel, OSPF will drop the adjacency.

Reference:
Cisco: OSPF Virtual Link: Using a GRE Tunnel Instead of a Virtual Link

QUESTION 10

You issue the show ip ospf neighbor command on a Cisco router. The router's OSPF neighbor state is FULL/DR. Which of the following is most likely true about the OSPF router? (Select the best answer.)

A.   It is the DR.
B.   It is the BDR.
• C.   It will exchange its entire database with the DR.
D.   It is on a pointtopoint network.

Correct Answer: (Look at the end of the book)

Explanation/Reference:
Explanation:

Most likely, the router will exchange its entire database with the designated router (DR) if the output of the show ip ospf neighbor command reveals that the router's Open Shortest Path First (OSPF) state is FULL/ DR. This output indicates that the router has formed a full adjacency with its neighbor and that the neighbor is the DR. This output also indicates that the router is configured on a multiaccess network because OSPF routers that are connected in a pointtopoint fashion do not elect a DR or BDR. The neighbor states for a multiaccess OSPF router include all of the following:

-        FULL/DR
-        FULL/BDR
-        2WAY/DROTHER

On a multiaccess network, OSPF routers exchange databases only with the DR and BDR, which helps prevent congestion. Therefore, routers with a 2WAY/ DROTHER state do not exchange full databases with those neighbors.

The router is not on a pointtopoint network. On a pointtopoint OSPF network, a neighbor state of FULL/indicates that the OSPF neighbors have formed a full adjacency and are thus capable of exchanging their entire databases. Because neither a DR nor a BDR exists on a pointtopoint network, the second field in the state output will be a dash.

The router is neither the DR nor the BDR. The first field in the state output indicates the state of the adjacency. The second field in the state indicates the type of OSPF router to which the router is connected, not the role of the router itself.

The DR generates linkstate advertisements (LSAs) that contain OSPF routing information, and the BDR takes over for the DR if the DR fails. Because only the DR and BDR generate LSAs, network bandwidth is conserved. The DR is typically the router with the highest OSPF priority, and the BDR is typically the router with the secondhighest OSPF priority. If priorities are equal between two or more routers, the router with the highest router ID will be elected. OSPF priorities can range from

0 through 255? the default OSPF priority is 1. A router with a priority of 0 will never become the DR or BDR. A router that is not the DR or BDR will display a state of DROTHER.

Reference:
Cisco: OSPF Neighbor Problems Explained: Typical Reasons for OSPF Neighbor Problems

QUESTION 11

Which of the following cannot be exchanged between spoke sites in a DMVPN design? (Select 2 choices.)

   A.   unicast traffic
   B.   multicast traffic
   C.   VoIP traffic
   D.   dynamic routing traffic

Correct Answer: (Look at the end of the book)

Explanation/Reference:
Explanation:
Multicast traffic and dynamic routing traffic cannot be exchanged between spoke sites in a Dynamic Multipoint virtual private network (DMVPN) design. Multicast traffic and dynamic routing traffic must be sent from spoke to hub.

DMVPN enables an administrator to easily configure scalable IP Security (IPSec) virtual private networks (VPNs) using a hubandspoke design. The hub router or routers are typically assigned a static IP address? the spoke routers can be dynamically addressed. DMVPN requires Generic Routing Encapsulation (GRE), Next Hop Resolution Protocol (NHRP), and a dynamic routing protocol such as Enhanced Interior Gateway Routing Protocol (EIGRP) or Open Shortest Path First (OSPF). A multipoint GRE (mGRE) tunnel is used to carry multiple IPSec or GRE tunnels. NHRP is used to create a database of tunnel addresstoreal address mappings.
Unicast traffic and Voice over IP (VoIP) traffic can be exchanged between spoke sites. However, only limited Quality of Service (QoS) mechanisms can be provided between spokes, thereby preventing VoIP and video traffic from being properly prioritized.

Reference:
Cisco: Multicast over IPSec VPN Design Guide: Overview
Cisco: Dynamic Multipoint VPN (DMVPN) Design Guide (Version 1.1): Known Limitations Summary for SpoketoSpoke Deployment Model (PDF)

QUESTION 12

RouterA and RouterB are connected routers.

You issue the show clns neighbors command on RouterA and receive the following output:

System Id	Interface	SNPA	State	Holdtime	…..	Type	Protocol
RouterB	Et0/0	0000.0000.000b	Up	23		L1	IS-IS

Which of the following statements must be true? (Select the best answer.)

* A.   RouterA and RouterB are in the same area.
   B.   RouterA and RouterB are in different areas.
   C.   RouterB is configured for L1 routing only.
   D.   RouterB is configured for L1/L2 routing.
   E.   RouterA is a backbone router.

Correct Answer: (Look at the end of the book)

Explanation/Reference:
Explanation:
RouterA and RouterB are in the same area. Routers running the Intermediate SystemtoIntermediate System (IS-IS) routing protocol are placed into administrative domains called areas. Each ISIS router resides in only one area. The collection of all areas managed by a single organization is called a routing domain.

Each ISIS router is configured with a routing level. Level 1 (L1) routers are capable of intraarea routing, which delivers data within a single area. The output of the show clns neighbors command indicates that RouterB has established an L1 adjacency with RouterA; therefore, both routers must be in the same area.

Level 2 (L2) routers are capable of interarea routing, which delivers data between areas. If RouterA and RouterB were in separate areas and both routers were configured for L2 routing, you would have received the following output from the show clns neighbors command:

System Id	Interface	SNPA	State		Holdtime
	Type Protocol RouterB Et0/0	0000.0000.000b	Up	23	L2
	IS-IS				

Level 1/Level 2 (L1/L2) routers are capable of both intraarea and interarea routing and maintain a separate linkstate database for each. If RouterA and RouterB were in the same area and both routers were configured for L1/L2 routing, you would have received the following output from the show clns neighbors command:

System Id	Interface	SNPA	State	Holdtime	Type
	Protocol				
RouterB	Et0/0	0000.0000.000b	Up	23	L1L2
	IS-IS				

You can configure the routing level for an ISIS process by issuing the istype {level1 | level12 | level2only} command, and you can configure the routing level for an ISIS interface by issuing the isis circuittype {level1 | level12 | level2only} command. By default, all ISIS routing processes and interfaces are configured for L1/ L2 routing.

RouterB is configured for either L1 routing or L1/L2 routing. However, the output of the show clns neighbors command in this scenario does not indicate which routing level RouterB is configured to use. If either router was configured for L1 routing only, the Typefield of the show clns neighbors command would show L1, even if the other router were an L1/L2 router.
The output of the show clns neighbors command in this scenario does not indicate whether RouterA is a backbone router. ISIS requires that all Level 2 (L2) and L1/ L2 routers be connected to form a backbone through the routing domain. If RouterA were configured for L1/L2 routing, RouterA would be a backbone router.

When an ISIS routing level mismatch, authentication mismatch, or maximum transmission unit (MTU) mismatch occurs, an ISIS adjacency will not form, but the output of the show clns neighbors command might instead show an End SystemtoIntermediate System (ESIS) adjacency. ESIS is used to discover end systems. If RouterA and RouterB were in different areas and if either router was configured for L1 routing only, you might see the following output after issuing the show clns neighbors command on RouterA:

System Id	Interface	SNPA	State	Holdtime	Type	Protocol
RouterB	Et0/0	0000.0000.000b	Up	23	IS	ES-IS

Reference:
Cisco: Cisco IOS ISO CLNS Command Reference: show clns neighbors

QUESTION 13

You issue the ip as-path access-list 1 permit ^7_23$ command on a BGP router.
Which of the following paths are allowed by the AS path filter? (Select the best answer.)

A.   paths that originate from AS 7 or AS 23
B.   paths that pass through AS 7 or AS 23
C.   paths that originate from AS 7 and are learned from AS 23

☞ D.   paths that are learned from AS 7 and originate from AS 23

Correct Answer: (Look at the end of the book)

Explanation/Reference:
Explanation:
Paths that are learned from Border Gateway Protocol (BGP) autonomous system (AS) 7 and originate from AS 23 are allowed by the AS path filter. Regular expressions are used to locate character strings that match a particular pattern.
The caret (^) character indicates that the subsequent characters should match the start of the string. Each router in the path prepends its AS number to the beginning of the AS path; therefore, the first AS number in the AS path is the AS from which the path is learned. Therefore, the ip aspath accesslist 1 permit ^7_23$ command allows paths that are learned from AS 7.

The dollar sign ($) character indicates that the preceding characters should match the end of the string. The originating router will insert its AS number into the AS path, and subsequent routers will prepend their AS numbers to the beginning of the AS path string. The last AS number in the AS path is the originating AS; therefore, the ip aspath accesslist 1 permit ^7_23$ command allows paths that originate from AS 23.

The underscore (_) character is used to indicate a comma, a brace, the start or end of an input string, or a space. When used between two AS path numbers, the _ character indicates that the ASes are directly connected. Therefore, the ip aspath accesslist 1 permit ^7_23$ command indicates that AS 7 is directly connected to AS 23.

The ip aspath accesslist 1 permit ^7_23$ command does not permit paths that originate from AS 7 and are learned from AS 23. To configure an AS path filter that

permits paths that originate from AS 7 and are learned from AS 23, you could issue the ip aspath accesslist 1 permit ^23_7$ command.

The ip aspath accesslist 1 permit ^7_23$ command does not permit paths that originate from AS 7 or AS 23; it only permits paths that originate from AS 23. To configure an AS path filter that permits paths that originate from AS 7 or AS 23, you could issue the following command set:

ip aspath accesslist 1 permit _7$ ip aspath accesslist 1 permit _23$

The ip aspath accesslist 1 permit ^7_23$ command does not permit paths that pass through AS 7 or AS 23. To configure an AS path filter that permits paths that pass through AS 7 or AS 23, you could issue the following command set:

ip aspath accesslist 1 permit _7_ ip aspath accesslist 1 permit _23_

Reference:
Cisco: Using Regular Expressions in BGP Cisco: Regular Expressions
Cisco: BGP Regular Expression AS Path Filter

QUESTION 14

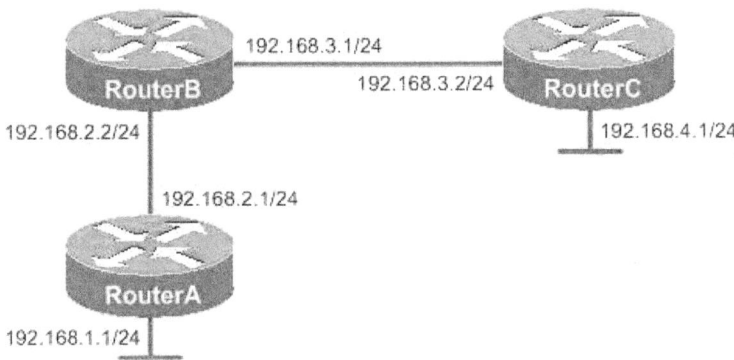

You administer the network shown above. RouterB and RouterC are running OSPF.
You issue the show ip ospf database external 192.168.1.0 command on RouterB and receive the following output:

```
OSPF Router with ID (192.168.3.1) (Process ID 20)
Type-5 AS External Link States
LS age: 42
Options: (NO TOS- capability, DC)
LS Type: AS External Link
Link State ID: 192.168.1.0 (External Network Number)
Advertising Router: 192.168.2.1
LS Seq Number: 80000001
Checksum: 0xF161
Length: 36
Network Mask: /24
          Metric Type: 2 (Larger than any link state path)
          TOS: 0
          Metric: 20
          Forward Address 192.168.2.1
          External Route Tag: 0
```

Which of the following statements is true about RouterB regarding the route to 192.168.1.0? (Select the best answer.)

* A.   The nexthop interface is running OSPF.
B.   The nexthop interface is passive.
C.   The nexthop interface is configured as a pointtopoint interface.
D.   RouterB is missing the network command for the 192.168.2.0 network.

Correct Answer: (Look at the end of the book)

Explanation/Reference:
Explanation:
The nexthop interface on RouterB is running Open Shortest Path First (OSPF). The output from the show ip ospf database external 192.168.1.0 command indicates that the forwarding address is 192.168.2.1. The forwarding address is a nonzero number only if the following five conditions are met:
-     OSPF is enabled on the nexthop interface.
-     The nexthop interface is not passive.
-     The nexthop interface is not pointtopoint.
-     The nexthop interface is not pointtomultipoint.
-     The nexthop interface address is a valid address within the subnet specified in the network command.

Therefore, the nexthop address must be running OSPF. If the

nexthop address were not running OSPF or if any of the above conditions were not met, the

forwarding address would be set to 0.0.0.0. This occurs because OSPF does not allow an external route to be used to reach another external OSPF route.

RouterB is not missing the network command for the 192.168.2.0 network. If it were, OSPF would not be enabled on the nexthop interface and the forwarding address would be set to 0.0.0.0. The next-hop interface is not set for point-to-point or point-to-multipoint operation. If it were, the forwarding address would be set to 0.0.0.0 and you would be required to issue a static route and to redistribute static and connected subnets.

The next-hop interface on RouterB is not passive. Configuring an interface as a passive interface prevents a router from sending or receiving OSPF routing information or hello packets on the specified interface. To configure a router as a passive interface, you should issue the passive-interface command in OSPF router configuration mode.

Reference:
Cisco: Common Routing Problem with OSPF Forwarding Address: Description of OSPF Forwarding Address

QUESTION 15

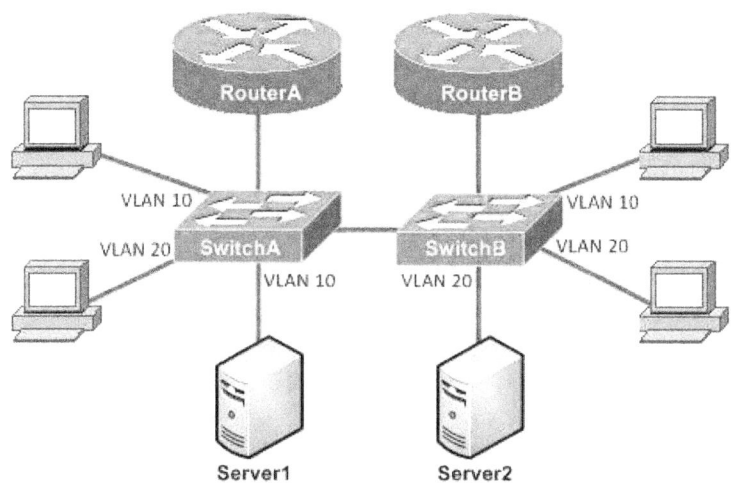

SwitchA and SwitchB are Layer 2 switches that are connected by a trunk link that forwards traffic for all VLANs. Server1 uses RouterA as its default gateway. Server2 uses RouterB as its default gateway. RouterA and RouterB are configured to perform interVLAN routing. Which of the following statements is true? (Select the best answer.)

A.   Server1 and Server2 will be unable to communicate.

B.   Server1 and Server2 will be able to communicate without any problems.

C.   Server1 will be able to communicate with Server2, but Server2 will not be able to communicate with Server1.

D.   Server2 will be able to communicate with Server1, but Server1 will not be able to communicate with Server2.

E.   Server1 and Server2 will be able to communicate, but excess unicast flooding will occur.

Correct Answer: (Look at the end of the book)

Explanation/Reference:
Explanation:
Server1 and Server2 will be able to communicate, but excess unicast flooding will occur because of asymmetric routing. When Server1 wants to communicate with Server2, Server1 sends the traffic

29

through SwitchA to its default gateway, RouterA. RouterA routes the traffic through the VLAN 20 subinterface to SwitchA. SwitchA does not know to which port Server2 is connected, so it floods the traffic to all ports that belong to VLAN 20. SwitchB receives the flooded traffic and forwards it directly to Server2.

When Server2 wants to respond to Server1, the same process happens in reverse. Server2 sends the traffic through SwitchB to its default gateway, RouterB. RouterB routes the traffic through the VLAN 10 subinterface to SwitchB. SwitchB does not know to which port Server1 is connected, so it floods the traffic to all ports that belong to VLAN 10. SwitchA receives the flooded traffic and forwards it directly to Server1.The behavior exhibited by the network topology in this scenario is called asymmetric routing. The excess unicast flooding occurs because SwitchA does not see traffic from the Media Access Control (MAC) address of Server2 and because SwitchB does not see traffic from the MAC address of Server1. When a switch receives traffic for a destination that is not listed in its forwarding table, it floods the traffic out all ports in that VLAN. If the servers in this scenario send a lot of traffic to one another, other devices connected to the switches can be adversely affected.

It is possible that one of the servers might send a broadcast Address Resolution Protocol (ARP) request, which will cause both switches to learn the MAC address of the server. This will cause the excess unicast flooding to stop. However, the server's MAC address will eventually age out of the forwarding table, and the excess unicast flooding will resume.

Reference:
https://www.cisco.com/c/en/us/support/docs/switches/catalyst-6000-series-switches/23563-143.html#causes

QUESTION 16

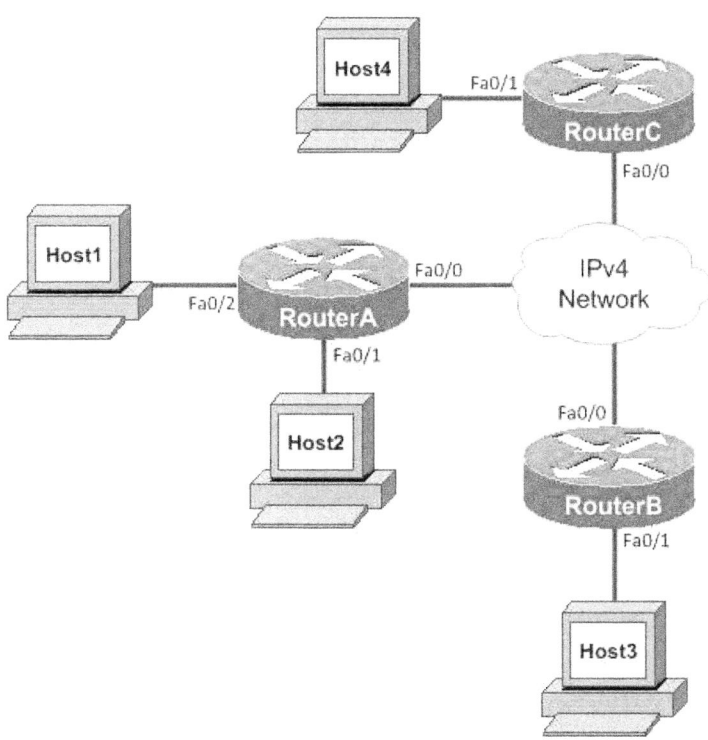

You administer the network shown in the diagram. You want to configure a 6to4 tunnel between RouterA and RouterB. You issue the show runningconfig command on RouterA and receive the following partial output:

interface FastEthernet 0/0
ip address 192.168.1.1 255.255.255.0

Which of the following command sets should you issue on RouterA? (Select the best answer.)

    A.   RouterA(config)#interface tunnel 0
            RouterA(configif)#ip address 192.168.1.1
            RouterA(configif)#tunnel source FastEthernet 0/0
            RouterA(configif)#tunnel mode ipv6ip 6to4
    B.   RouterA(config)#interface tunnel 0
          RouterA(configif)#ip address 192.168.1.1
          RouterA(configif)#tunnel source 2002:C0A8:0101::1/64

RouterA(configif)#tunnel mode 6to4

● C.   RouterA(config)#interface tunnel 0
RouterA(configif)#ipv6 address 2002:C0A8:0101::1/64
RouterA(configif)#tunnel source FastEthernet 0/0
RouterA(configif)#tunnel mode ipv6ip 6to4
RouterA(configif)#exit
RouterA(config)#ipv6 route 2002::/16 tunnel 0

D.   RouterA(config)#interface tunnel 0
RouterA(configif)#ipv6 address 2002:C0A8:0101::1/64
RouterA(configif)#tunnel mode 6to4
RouterA(configif)#exit
RouterA(config)#ipv6 route 2002::/16 tunnel 0

Correct Answer: (Look at the end of the book)

Explanation/Reference:
Explanation:
You should issue the following commands on RouterA:

RouterA(config)#interface tunnel 0
RouterA(configif)#ipv6 address 2002:C0A8:0101::1/64
RouterA(configif)#tunnel source FastEthernet 0/0
RouterA(configif)#tunnel mode ipv6ip 6to4
RouterA(configif)#exit
RouterA(config)#ipv6 route 2002::/16 tunnel 0

First, you should create the tunnel by issuing the interface tunnel
tunnel number command. Issuing the interface tunnel 0 command
will create the Tunnel 0 interface and place the router in interface
configuration mode.

Next, you should assign an IPv6 address for the tunnel by issuing the
ipv6 address ipv6 address command. The IPv6 address for a 6to4
tunnel interface begins with 2002::/16, and the 32 bits following the
2002::/16 prefix correspond to the IPv4 address of the tunnel source.
To calculate the IPv6 address prefix that should be used for the
tunnel, you should convert the IPv4 address of the tunnel source
from dotted decimal to hexadecimal and append it to the 2002::/16
prefix. In this scenario, the tunnel source is the IPv4 address of the

FastEthernet 0/0 interface, which is 192.168.1.1. The dotted decimal address 192.168.1.1 converts to the hexadecimal address C0A8:0101. Therefore, the IPv6 address prefix 2002:C0A8:0101::/64 should be used for the tunnel? the IPv6 address 2002:C0A8:0101::1/64 is a valid host address for this prefix.

Alternatively, you can have the tunnel use the IPv6 address that is configured for another router interface by issuing the ipv6 unnumbered interface command. However, for a 6to4 tunnel, the interface must be configured with an IPv6 address that corresponds to the IPv4 address of the tunnel source.

Next, you should configure the tunnel source by issuing the tunnel source {ipv4address | interface} command. In this scenario, you should issue either the tunnel source 192.168.1.1 command or the tunnel source FastEthernet 0/0 command.
You should then configure the tunnel mode for 6to4 operation by issuing the tunnel mode ipv6ip 6to4 command. The following tunnel mode commands can be used for IPv6 overlay tunnel creation:
-        tunnel mode ipv6ip 6to4 - creates a 6to4 tunnel
-        tunnel mode ipv6ip - creates a manual IPv6 tunnel
-        tunnel mode gre ipv6 - creates a Generic Routing Encapsulation (GRE) tunnel
-        tunnel mode ipv6ip autotunnel- creates an IPv4compatible tunnel
-tunnel mode ipv6ip isatap - creates an IntraSite Automatic Tunnel Addressing Protocol (ISATAP) tunnel

The complete procedure for setting up an IPv6 tunnel differs for each of the tunnel types listed above.

Finally, you should exit interface configuration mode and configure a static route to direct IPv6 traffic to the 6to4 tunnel by issuing the ipv6 route ipv6prefix/ prefixlength tunnel tunnelnumber command in global configuration mode. The prefix 2002::/16 must always be used for 6to4 tunnels.

After you have issued the commands to create the tunnel on RouterA, you should issue similar commands on RouterB to create the other side of the tunnel. The following command set is incorrect because an IPv6 address, not an IPv4 address, should be configured for the tunnel:

RouterA(config)#interface tunnel 0
RouterA(configif)#ip address 192.168.1.1
RouterA(configif)#tunnel source FastEthernet 0/0
RouterA(configif)#tunnel mode ipv6ip 6to4

Additionally, the ipv6 route 2002::/16 tunnel 0 command is missing. The following command set is incorrect because an IPv6 address, not an IPv4 address, should be configured for the tunnel:
RouterA(config)#interface tunnel 0
RouterA(configif)#ip address 192.168.1.1
 RouterA(configif)#tunnel source 2002:C0A8:0101::1/64
RouterA(configif)#tunnel mode 6to4

Additionally, the tunnel source should specify an IPv4 address or an IPv4enabled interface, not an IPv6 address. Furthermore, the tunnel mode 6to4 command is not a valid Cisco command. Finally, the ipv6 route 2002::/16 tunnel 0 command is missing.
The following command set is incorrect because the tunnel mode is incorrectly specified by the tunnel mode 6to4 command:

RouterA(config)#interface tunnel 0
RouterA(configif)#ipv6 address 2002:C0A8:0101::1/64

RouterA(configif)#tunnel source 192.168.1.1
RouterA(configif)#tunnel mode 6to4 RouterA(configif)#exit
RouterA(config)#ip route 2002::/16 tunnel 0

Although the tunnel source 192.168.1.1 command in this command set is specified differently from the tunnel source FastEthernet 0/0 command in the correct command set, both are valid methods of specifying the tunnel source.

Reference:
Cisco: Implementing Tunneling for IPv6

QUESTION 17

Which of the following are benefits of using VRRP? (Select 3 choices.)

A.   VRRP supports up to 1,024 virtual routers per physical router interface.
* B.   VRRP provides one virtual IP address for a group of routers.
* C.   VRRP can be used with routers from different vendors.
D.   VRRP allows load balancing across multiple WAN links.
* E.   VRRP supports MD5 authentication.

Correct Answer: (Look at the end of the book)

Explanation/Reference:
Explanation:
Virtual Router Redundancy Protocol (VRRP) provides one virtual IP address for a group of routers, VRRP can be used with routers from different vendors, and VRRP supports Message Digest 5 (MD5) authentication. VRRP is a standardsbased protocol that enables a group of routers to form a single virtual router. With VRRP, several routers are grouped to appear like a single default gateway for the network. VRRP uses the IP address of a physical interface on the master virtual router, which is the router in the group with the highest VRRP priority. The other routers in the group are known as backup virtual routers. If the master virtual router fails, the backup virtual router with the highest priority will assume the role of the master virtual router, thereby providing uninterrupted service for the network. When the original master virtual router comes back online, it reestablishes its role as the master virtual router.
Because VRRP is a standardsbased protocol, VRRP can be used with routers from many different vendors. VRRP is defined in Request for Comments (RFC)

3768. By contrast, Hot Standby Router Protocol (HSRP) and Gateway Load Balancing Protocol (GLBP) are both Ciscoproprietary protocols. Therefore, HSRP and GLBP cannot be used with routers from multiple vendors.
VRRP supports plaintext and MD5 authentication. When a router

receives a VRRP packet for its VRRP group, it validates the authentication string. If the authentication string does not match the string that is configured on the router, the VRRP packet is discarded. When plaintext authentication is configured, the authentication string is sent unencrypted. When MD5 authentication is configured, each VRRP packet is sent with a keyed MD5 hash of that packet? if the receiving device does not generate the same hash, the packet is ignored.

Because only the VRRP master virtual router can be the default gateway, VRRP does not allow load balancing across multiple WAN links. By contrast, GLBP allows up to four primary active virtual forwarders (AVFs) to load balance across multiple WAN links. The virtual router has its own virtual IP address and up to four virtual Media Access Control (MAC) addresses, one for each of the primary AVFs in the group. One of the routers in the GLBP group is elected the active virtual gateway (AVG) and performs the administrative tasks for the standby group, such as responding to Address Resolution Protocol (ARP) requests. When a client sends an ARP request for the IP address of the default gateway, the AVG responds with one of the virtual MAC addresses in the group. Because multiple routers in the GLBP group can actively forward traffic, GLBP provides load balancing as well as local redundancy.GLBP, not VRRP, can support up to 1,024 virtual routers per physical router interface. VRRP and HSRP both support up to 255 virtual routers per physical router interface.

Reference:
https://www.cisco.com/c/en/us/td/docs/ios-xml/ios/ipapp_fhrp/configuration/12-4/fhp-12-4-book/fhp-vrrp.html https://www.cisco.com/c/en/us/td/docs/ios-xml/ios/ipapp_fhrp/command/fhp-cr-book/fhp-v1.html#wp8990239320

QUESTION 18

You want to establish an EtherChannel between SwitchA and SwitchB.
Which of the following modes can you configure on both of the switches to establish the EtherChannel over PAgP? (Select the best

answer.)

A.   on
B.   passive
C.   active
● D.   desirable
E.   auto

Correct Answer: (Look at the end of the book)

Explanation/Reference:
Explanation:
You can configure both switches to operate in desirable mode to establish the EtherChannel over Port Aggregation Protocol (PAgP). Alternatively, you can set one switch to auto and the other switch to desirable.

PAgP is a Ciscoproprietary protocol that groups individual physical PAgPconfigured ports into a single logical link, called an EtherChannel. The ports that constitute an EtherChannel are grouped according to various parameters, such as hardware, port, and administrative limitations. Once PAgP has created an EtherChannel, it adds the EtherChannel to the spanning tree as a single switch port. Because PAgP is a Cisco-proprietary protocol, it can be used only on Cisco switches.

Link Aggregation Control Protocol (LACP) is a newer, standardsbased alternative to PAgP that is defined by the Institute of Electrical and Electronics Engineers (IEEE) 802.3ad standard. LACP is available on switches newer than the Catalyst 2950 switch, which offers only PAgP. Like PAgP, LACP identifies neighboring ports and their group capabilities; however, LACP goes further by assigning roles to the EtherChannel's endpoints. Because LACP is a standardsbased protocol, it can be used between Cisco and nonCisco switches.

The following table displays the channelgroup configurations that will establish an EtherChannel:

SwitchB SwitchA	off	auto	desirable	passive	active	on
off	NO	NO	NO	NO	NO	NO
auto	NO	NO	PAgP	NO	NO	NO
desirable	NO	PAgP	PAgP	NO	NO	NO
passive	NO	NO	NO	NO	LACP	NO
active	NO	NO	NO	LACP	LACP	NO
on	NO	NO	NO	NO	NO	ON

The channelgroup command configures the EtherChannel mode.
The syntax of the channelgroup command is channelgroup number
mode {on | active | passive | {auto | desirable} [nonsilent]}, where
number is the port channel interface number. The on keyword
configures the channel group to unconditionally create the channel
with no LACP or PAgP negotiation.

The active and passive keywords can be used only with LACP. The
active keyword configures the channel group to actively negotiate
LACP, and the passive keyword configures the channel group to
listen for LACP negotiation to be offered. Either or both sides of the
link must be set to active to establish an EtherChannel over LACP?
setting both sides to passive will not establish an EtherChannel over
LACP.

The auto, desirable, and nonsilent keywords can be used only with
PAgP. The desirable keyword configures the channel group to
actively negotiate PAgP, and the autokeyword configures the channel
group to listen for PAgP negotiation to be offered. Either or both
sides of the link must be set to desirable to establish an EtherChannel
over PAgP; setting both sides to auto will not establish an
EtherChannel over PAgP. The optional nonsilent keyword requires
that a port receive PAgP packets before the port is added to the
channel.

Reference:
https://www.cisco.com/c/en/us/support/docs/switches/catalyst-
4000-series-switches/23408-140.html#lacp_pagp
https://www.cisco.com/c/en/us/td/docs/switches/lan/catalyst375
0/software/release/12-
2_52_se/command/reference/3750cr/cli1.html#wp11890010
https://www.cisco.com/c/en/us/td/docs/switches/lan/catalyst375
0/software/release/12-

2_52_se/command/reference/3750cr/cli1.html#wp11890203

QUESTION 19

Which of the following statements are true regarding OSPFv3? (Select 3 choices.)

A.   OSPFv3 does not support IPv6.
* B.   Enabling OSPFv3 on an interface enables the OSPFv3 routing process on the router.

C.   Network addresses are included in the OSPFv3 process when the network command is issued.
D.   OSPFv3 sends hello messages and LSAs over multicast addresses 224.0.0.5 and 224.0.0.6.
* E.   The BDR is elected before the DR is elected.
F.   OSPFv3 uses MD5 to secure communication.
* G.   OSPFv3 supports multiple instances on a single link.

Correct Answer: (Look at the end of the book)

Explanation/Reference:
Explanation:
Enabling Open Shortest Path First version 3 (OSPFv3) on an interface enables the OSPFv3 routing process on the router. Additionally, the backup designated router (BDR) is elected before the designated router (DR) is elected. Finally, OSPFv3 supports multiple instances on a link. To enable OSPFv3 on an interface, you should issue the ipv6 ospf processid area areaid command in interface configuration mode. To enter router configuration mode for OSPFv3, you should issue the ipv6 router ospf processid command or the router ospfv3 [processid] command in global configuration mode.
The DR and BDR election process for OSPFv3 multiaccess segments is handled the same way as it is handled in OSPFv2: the BDR is elected first, and then the DR is elected. The router with the highest priority, as long as it has not already declared itself as the DR, becomes the BDR. Of those routers that have declared themselves as

the DR, the router with the highest priority is elected to become the DR. If priority values are equal, the router with the highest router ID is elected. To change the OSPF priority of a router, you should issue the ip ospf priority value command, where value is an integer from 0 through 255. The default OSPF priority is 1, and a router with an OSPF priority of 0 will never be elected the DR or BDR. OSPFv3 supports both IPv4 and IPv6. OSPFv3, which is described in Request for Comments (RFC) 2740, was developed as an enhancement to OSPFv2, which supports only IPv4. An OSPFv3 instance can support either IPv4 or IPv6, but not both. However, you can run multiple OSPFv3 instances on a single link. You can issue the ospfv3 processid area areaid {ipv4 | ipv6} [instance instanceid] command to enable OSPFv3 on an interface for a particular address family.

Network addresses are not included in the OSPFv3 process when the network command is issued. The network command is not required, because OSPFv3 is configured directly on each participating interface. Each IPv6 interface is designed to be configured with many different types of IPv6 addresses, such as sitelocal, linklocal, and global unicast. When you configure OSPFv3 on an interface, all IPv6 address prefixes are included? you cannot exclude certain prefixes and allow others.OSPFv3 does not send hello messages or linkstate advertisements (LSAs) over the IPv4 multicast addresses 224.0.0.5 and 224.0.0.6. Instead, OSPFv3 uses the IPv6 multicast addresses FF02::5 and FF02::6. All OSPFv3 routers receive packets destined for FF02::5, which is similar to the OSPFv2 allrouters multicast address 224.0.0.5. OSPFv3 DRs and BDRs receive packets destined for FF02::6, which is similar to the OSPFv2 allDR/BDR multicast address 224.0.0.6. Unlike OSPFv2, OSPFv3 does not use Message Digest 5 (MD5) to secure communication. Instead, OSPFv3 uses IP Security (IPSec) to secure communication.

Reference:
https://search.cisco.com/search?query=Cisco%20IOS%20IPv6%20Configuration%20Guide&locale=enUS&tab=Cisco
http://www.ietf.org/rfc/rfc2328.txt
http://www.ietf.org/rfc/rfc2740.txt
https://www.cisco.com/c/en/us/td/docs/ios-xml/ios/iproute_ospf/configuration/15-sy/iro-15-sy-book/ip6-

route-ospfv3-esp.html

QUESTION 20

You administer the network in the following exhibit:

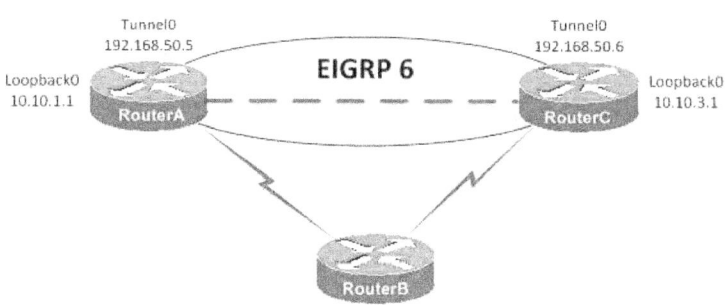

You issue the show runningconfig command on RouterA and receive the following partial output:

interface Loopback0
ip address 10.10.1.1 255.255.255.0
!
interface Tunnel0
ip address 192.168.50.5 255.255.255.0
tunnel source Loopback0 tunnel destination 10.10.3.1

RouterA and RouterC are both configured to use RouterB as a gateway of last resort. Additionally, static routes to the Loopback0 interfaces on RouterA and RouterC have beenconfigured on RouterB.

You configure EIGRP on RouterA and then issue the show ip route command, which produces the following partial output: Gateway of last resort is 172.15.1.2 to network 0.0.0.0
172.15.0.0/24 is subnetted, 1 subnets
C 172.15.1.0 is directly connected, Serial0/0 10.0.0.0/24 is subnetted, 2 subnets
10.10.1.0 is directly connected, Loopback0

10.10.3.0 [90/297372416] via 192.168.50.6, 00:00:01, Tunnel0
C 192.168.50.0/24 is directly connected, Tunnel0 S* 0.0.0.0/0 [1/0]
via 172.15.1.2

Which of the following is true? (Select the best answer.)

A.   The Tunnel0 interface and EIGRP adjacency on RouterA will
flap.
B.   The Tunnel0 interface and EIGRP adjacency on RouterA will
function properly.
C.   The Tunnel0 interface on RouterA will function properly, but
EIGRP will flap.
D.   The Tunnel0 interface on RouterA will flap, but the EIGRP
adjacency will function properly.

Correct Answer: (Look at the end of the book)

Explanation/Reference:
Explanation:
The Tunnel0 interface and Enhanced Interior Gateway Routing
Protocol (EIGRP) adjacency on RouterA will flap because the
preferred route to the Tunnel0 destination interface is through the
tunnel itself, which results in recursive routing. When recursive
routing occurs, the Tunnel0 interfaces on both RouterA and RouterC
will be temporarily disabled, which breaks the EIGRP adjacency.
The EIGRP adjacency will reestablish when the tunnel interfaces
return to the up state. Therefore, if you were to issue the show ip
route command on RouterA while the adjacency is established, you
would see that the preferred route to the Loopback0 interface on
RouterC from RouterA is through Tunnel0, even though the
destination interface for Tunnel0 on RouterA is the Loopback0
interface on RouterC.
If the cause of the recursive routing is not fixed, the Tunnel0
interfaces will flap and errorssimilar to the following will be displayed
on RouterA:

*Mar 1 00:26:15.379: %TUN5RECURDOWN: Tunnel0 temporarily
disabled due to recursive routing
*Mar 1 00:26:16.379: %LINEPROTO5UPDOWN: Line protocol on

Interface Tunnel0, changed state to down
*Mar 1 00:26:16.487: %DUAL5NBRCHANGE: IPEIGRP(0) 6:
Neighbor 192.168.50.6 (Tunnel0) is down: interface down

In this scenario, an EIGRP adjacency has been established between
the Tunnel0 interfaceson RouterA and RouterC. When the EIGRP
adjacency comes up, the show ip route command displays Tunnel0 as
the preferred route to 192.168.50.0 instead of the gateway of last
resort. Therefore, the EIGRP 6 domain has been configured to
include the 10.10.1.0/24 and 192.168.50.0/24 networks on RouterA
and the 10.10.3.0/24 and 192.168.50.0/24 networks on RouterC. As
a result, recursive routing to the 10.10.3.0 network through Tunnel0
occurs on RouterA and recursive routing to the 10.10.1.0 network
occurs on RouterC.

There are two ways to resolve the recursive routing issue on both
RouterA and RouterC in this scenario: remove the 192.168.50.0/24
network from the EIGRP 6 domain, or add a static route to the
Tunnel0 destination IP addresses on both RouterA and RouterC. A
static route has a lower administrative distance (AD) than EIGRP.
Therefore, a static route would fix the recursive routing problem.

Reference:
https://www.cisco.com/c/en/us/support/docs/ip/enhanced-
interior-gateway-routing-protocol-eigrp/22327-gre-flap.html

QUESTION 21

In a three-node OpenStack architecture, the network node consists
of services from which of the following OpenStack components?
(Select the best answer.)

A.   Glance

B.   Horizon
C.   Keystone
♦ D.   Neutron
E.   Nova

Correct Answer: (Look at the end of the book)

Explanation/Reference:
Explanation:
In a three-node OpenStack architecture, the network node consists of services from the Neutron component. OpenStack is an open-source cloud-computing platform. Each OpenStack modular component is responsible for a particular function, and each component has a code name. The following list contains several of the most popular OpenStack components:

-Nova -OpenStack Compute: manages pools of computer resources
-Neutron -OpenStack Networking: manages networking and addressing
-Cinder -OpenStack Block Storage: manages blocklevel storage devices
-Glance -OpenStack Image: manages disk and server images
-Swift -OpenStack Object Storage: manages redundant storage systems
-Keystone -OpenStack Identity: is responsible for authentication
-Horizon -OpenStack Dashboard: provides a graphical user interface (GUI)
-Ceilometer -OpenStackTelemetry: provides counterbased tracking that can be used for customer usage billing

A three-node OpenStack architecture consists of the network node, the controller node, and the compute node. The network node consists of the following Neutron services:

-Neutron Modular Layer 2 (ML2) PlugIn
-Neutron Layer 2 Agent
-Neutron Layer 3 Agent
-Neutron Dynamic Host Configuration Protocol (DHCP) Agent The controller node consists of the following services:
-Keystone
-Glance
-Nova Management
-Neutron Server
-Neutron ML2 Plug-In

-Horizon
-Cinder

-Swift
-Ceilometer Core

The compute node consists of the following services:

-Nova Hypervisor
-Kernel-based Virtual Machine (KVM) or Quick Emulator (QEMU)
-Neutron ML2 Plug-In
-Neutron Layer 2 Agent
-Ceilometer Agent

Reference:
https://www.redhat.com/archives/rdo-list/2014-
November/pdfzGvyHATdWc.pdf#page=12

QUESTION 22

Which of the following routing protocols can be used for routing on
IoT networks? (Select the best answer.)

A.   EIGRP
B.   IS-IS
C.   OSPF
D.   RPL

Correct Answer: (Look at the end of the book)

Explanation/Reference:
Explanation:
Routing Protocol for Lowpower and Lossy Networks (RPL) can be
used for routing on Internet of Things (IoT) networks. RPL is an IP
version 6 (IPv6) routing protocol that is defined in Request for
Comments (RFC) 6550. An IoT network is considered to be a Lowpower and Lossy Network (LLN).
IoT networks connect embedded devices. Embedded devices, or
smart objects, are typically lowpower, lowmemory devices with

limited processing capabilities. These devices are used in a variety of applications, such as environmental monitoring, healthcare monitoring, process automation, and location tracking. Many embedded devices can transmit data wirelessly, and some are capable of transmitting over a wired connection. However, connectivity is generally unreliable and bandwidth is often constrained.

IoT networks require a routing protocol that can handle the limitations of embedded devices. Neither Enhanced Interior Gateway Routing Protocol (EIGRP), Intermediate SystemtoIntermediate System (IS-IS), nor Open Shortest Path First (OSPF) meets the requirements for routing an IoT network, as specified by the Internet Engineering Task Force (IETF) Routing over LLNs (ROLL) working group. In addition to RPL, IPv6 over Low Power Wireless Personal Area Networks (6LoWPAN) and Constrained Application Protocol (CoAP) have been created to address the challenges of routing an IoT network.

Reference: https://tools.ietf.org/html/rfc6550

https://datatracker.ietf.org/wg/roll/charter/

QUESTION 23

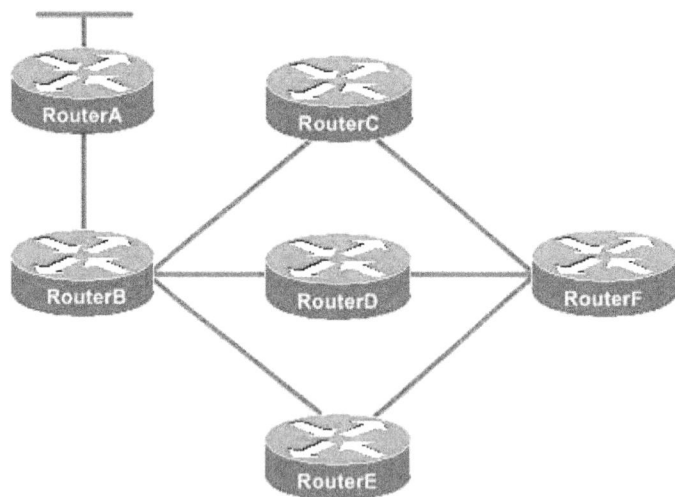

You administer the EIGRP network shown above. RouterB is configured to send only a summary route to RouterE. RouterC is

configured as a stub router. The link between RouterA and RouterB
fails.
Which of the following routers will send a query to RouterF? (Select
the best answer.)

A.   only RouterC
▪ B.   only RouterD
C.   only RouterE
D.   only RouterC and RouterD
E.   only RouterD and RouterE
F.   RouterC, RouterD, and RouterE

Correct Answer: (Look at the end of the book)

Explanation/Reference:
Explanation:
Only RouterD will send a query to RouterF. Query packets are sent
to find routes to a destination network. When a router loses the best
route to a destination and does not have a feasible successor, it floods
query packets to its neighbors. If a neighbor has a route to the
destination network, it replies with the route. However, if a neighbor
does not have a route to the destination network, it queries its
neighbors, those neighbors query their neighbors, and so on. This
process continues until either a router replies with the route or there
are no routers left to query. The network cannot converge until all
the replies have been received, which can cause a router to become
stuck in active (SIA).
Limiting Enhanced Interior Gateway Routing Protocol (EIGRP)
queries prevents queries from consuming bandwidth and processor
resources and prevents routers from becoming SIA. You can display
which routers have not yet replied to a query by issuing the show ip
eigrp topology active command, as shown in the following output:

```
RouterA#show ip eigrp topology active
IP-EIGRP Topology Table for AS(1)/ID(192.168.99.2)

Codes: P - Passive, A - Active, U - Update, Q - Query, R - Reply,
       r - reply Status, s - sia Status

A: 192.168.99.3/32, 1 successors, FD is Inaccessible, tag is 1
   1 replies, active 00:05:15, query-origin: Local origin
       via Redistributed (2297856/0)
     Remaining replies:
       via 192.168.99.3, r, Serial0/0.223
```

The eigrp stub command limits EIGRP queries by creating a stub router. Stub routers advertise only a specified set of routes and therefore typically need only a default route from a hub router. A hub router detects that a router is a stub router by examining the Type-Length-Value (TLV) field within EIGRP hello packets sent by the router. The hub router will specify in its neighbor table that the router is a stub router and will no longer send query packets to that stub router, thereby limiting how far EIGRP queries spread throughout a network. Because RouterC is configured as a stub router, RouterB will not send queries to RouterC, and RouterC will therefore not propagate those queries to RouterF. Although hub routers will not send queries to stub routers, stub routers can initiate queries of their own.

The ip summary address eigrp as number address mask command limits EIGRP queries by configuring route summarization. If a neighbor router has a summarized route but does not have the specific route to the destination network in the query, the neighbor router will reply that it does not have a route to the destination network and will not query its neighbors. Thus route summarization creates a query boundary that prevents queries from propagating throughout the network. In this scenario, RouterB is configured to send only a summary route to RouterE; therefore, RouterE will not send queries to RouterF.

RouterD is not configured as a stub router, and RouterB is not sending RouterD a summarized route. Therefore, when RouterB sends a query to RouterD, RouterD will send a query to RouterF.

Reference:
https://www.cisco.com/en/US/technologies/tk648/tk365/technolo
gies_white_paper0900aecd8023df6f.html

48

QUESTION 24

What is the size of the IPv6 fragment header? (Select the best answer.)

A.   32 bits
B.   64 bits
C.   20 bytes
D.   40 bytes
E.   1,280 bytes

Correct Answer: (Look at the end of the book)

Explanation/Reference:
Explanation:
The IPv6 fragment header is 64 bits long. The fragment header is used by an IPv6 source to indicate a packet that exceeds the path maximum transmission unit (MTU) size. Unlike IPv4, which enables intervening devices such as routers to fragment packets that exceed the permitted size for a local link, IPv6 requires the traffic originator to ensure that each packet sent is small enough to traverse the entire link without fragmentation. The packet can then be reassembled at the destination.
The IPv6 fragment header is not 32 bits long. However, the IPv6 fragment header contains a 32bit field called the identification field. The identification field is used to uniquely identify each fragmented packet.
The IPv6 fragment header is neither 20 bytes nor 40 bytes long. A basic IPv4 header without options is 20 bytes long, and a basic IPv6 header without extension headers is 40 bytes long. Although an IPv4 header is shorter than an IPv6 header, it is more complex and contains more fields than an IPv6 header. Several fields that exist in an IPv4 header, such as the Header Checksum field and the Fragment Offset field, do not exist in an IPv6 header. Because many protocols at the Data Link and Transport layers contain mechanisms to verify the integrity of the packet, IPv6 does not contain a redundant method to calculate checksum values.
The IPv6 fragment header is not 1,280 bytes long. The default IPv6

MTU size is 1,280 bytes. IPv6 requires that each device have an MTU of 1,280 bytes or greater.

Reference: https://www.ietf.org/rfc/rfc2460.txt

QUESTION 25

Which of the following mutual redistribution scenarios does not require you to configure manual redistribution? (Select the best answer.)

A.   static routes and RIPv2
B.   static routes and EIGRP
C.   OSPF processes with different process IDs
D.   IS-IS and OSPF processes with the same area number
E.   IGRP and EIGRP processes with the same ASN
F.   EIGRP processes with different ASNs

Correct Answer: (Look at the end of the book)

Explanation/Reference:
Explanation:
Interior Gateway Routing Protocol (IGRP) processes and Enhanced IGRP (EIGRP) processes with the same autonomous system number (ASN) do not require manual redistribution. Mutual redistribution of IGRP and EIGRP routing processes occurs automatically if the processes share the same ASN; there is no additional configuration required to enable route redistribution between the IGRP and EIGRP processes. However, you must manually configure route redistribution between IGRP and EIGRP processes with different ASNs.
Routing Information Protocol version 2 (RIPv2) automatically redistributes static routes that point to an interface on the router. However, RIP does not redistribute static routes that point to a nexthop IP address unless you issue the redistribute static command from RIP router configuration mode. RIPv2 assigns static routes a metric of 1 and redistributes them as though they were directly

connected. Because there is only one routing protocol involved when static routes are redistributed into a RIPv2 routing domain, this is a one way redistribution of routing information.

EIGRP automatically redistributes static routes that point to an interface on the router.

However, EIGRP does not redistribute static routes that point to a nexthop IP addressunless you issue the redistribute static command from EIGRP router configuration mode. The static route is redistributed as an external route. Because there is only one routing protocol involved when static routes are redistributed into an EIGRP routing domain, this is a oneway redistribution of routing information.

Open Shortest Path First (OSPF) processes with different process IDs do not redistribute routes without manual configuration. Although it is possible to run multiple OSPF processes on a single router, it is not recommended, because suboptimal routing and routing loops may occur.

Intermediate System-to-Intermediate System (IS-IS) and OSPF processes with the same area number do not redistribute routes without manual configuration. ISIS and OSPF both assign a default metric to redistributed routes unless otherwise specified.

Reference:
https://www.cisco.com/c/en/us/support/docs/ip/enhanced-interior-gateway-routing-protocol-eigrp/16406-eigrp-toc.html#sameauto
https://www.cisco.com/c/en/us/support/docs/ip/enhanced-interior-gateway-routing-protocol-eigrp/8606-redist.html

QUESTION 26

You are considering moving your company's software development to a public cloudbased solution. Which of the following are least likely to increase? (Select 2 choices.)

A.   availability
B.   redundancy
C.   security ✳
D.   mobility

E.   control ✘
F.   scalability

Correct Answer: (Look at the end of the book)

Explanation/Reference:
Explanation:
Of the choices provided, security and control are least likely to increase. With a public cloudbased solution, the service provider, not the customer, controls the cloud infrastructure and devices. Therefore, physical security of the data and hardware is no longer in the customer's control. In addition, resources stored in the public cloud are typically accessed over the Internet. Care must be taken so that the data can be accessed securely.
Availability, redundancy, mobility, and scalability are all likely to increase by moving to a public cloudbased solution. Cloudbased resources are typically spread over several devices, sometimes even in multiple geographic areas, thereby ensuring availability. If one device or location becomes unavailable, other devices and locations can handle the workload. Data stored on cloudbased resources can be copied or moved to other devices or locations, thereby increasing redundancy and mobility. As usage increases, additional devices can be brought online, thereby providing scalability.

Reference:
https://www.cisco.com/c/en/us/about/press/internet-protocol-journal/back-issues/table-contents-45/123-cloud1.html

QUESTION 27

In a threenode OpenStack architecture, which services are part of the compute node? (Select 2 choices.)

A.   Ceilometer Agent •
B.   Ceilometer Core
C.   Neutron DHCP Agent
D.   Neutron Server
E.   Nova Hypervisor ▪

F.   Nova Management
G.   Correct

Correct Answer: (Look at the end of the book)

Explanation/Reference:
Explanation:
In a three-node OpenStack architecture, the Ceilometer Agent and the Nova Hypervisorservices are part of the compute node. OpenStack is an opensource cloudcomputing platform. Each OpenStack modular component is responsible for a particular function, and each component has a code name. The following list contains several of the most popular OpenStack components:

-Nova -OpenStack Compute: manages pools of computer resources
-Neutron -OpenStack Networking: manages networking and addressing
-Cinder -OpenStack Block Storage: manages blocklevel storage devices
-Glance -OpenStack Image: manages disk and server images
-Swift -OpenStack Object Storage: manages redundant storage systems

-Keystone -OpenStack Identity: is responsible for authentication
-Horizon -OpenStack Dashboard: provides a graphical user interface (GUI)
-Ceilometer -OpenStackTelemetry: provides counterbased tracking that can be used   for customer usage billing

A threenode OpenStack architecture consists of the compute node, the controller node, and the network node. The compute node consists of the following services:

-Nova Hypervisor
-Kernelbased Virtual Machine (KVM) or Quick Emulator (QEMU)
-Neutron Modular Layer 2 (ML2) PlugIn
-Neutron Layer 2 Agent
-Ceilometer Agent
-The controller node consists of the following services:

-Keystone
-Glance
-Nova Management
-Neutron Server
-Neutron ML2 PlugIn
-Horizon
-Cinder
-Swift
-Ceilometer Core

The network node consists of several Neutron services:

-Neutron ML2 PlugIn
-Neutron Layer 2 Agent
-Neutron Layer 3 Agent
-Neutron Dynamic Host Configuration Protocol (DHCP) Agent

Reference:
https://www.redhat.com/archives/rdo-list/2014-
November/pdfzGvyHATdWc.pdf#page=12

QUESTION 28

You issue the show runningconfig command on RouterA and receive
the following partial output:

```
class-map voip
  match ip dscp ef
class-map video
  match ip dscp 41
class-map ftp
  match protocol ftp
policy-map boson
  class voip
    priority percent 20
  class video
    bandwidth percent 40
  class ftp
    bandwidth remaining-percent 50
  class class-default
    bandwidth remaining-percent 25
!
interface FastEthernet0/1
  ip address 10.20.30.1 255.255.255.0
max-reserved-bandwidth 100
  service-policy output boson
```

Ho much web traffic can RouterA send out the FastEthernet0/1
interface during periods of heavy voice and video traffic? (Select the
best answer.)

A.   10 Mbps
B.   15 Mbps
C.   20 Mbps
D.   25 Mbps
E.   40 Mbps

Correct Answer: (Look at the end of the book)

Explanation/Reference:
Explanation:
RouterA can send 10 Mbps of web traffic out the FastEthernet0/1
interface during periods of heavy voice and video traffic. To create a
Quality of Service (QoS)

policy, you must perform the following steps:

1.   Define one or more class maps by issuing the classmap name
command.

55

2.   Define the traffic that matches the class map by issuing one or more match commands. 3.Define one or more policy maps by issuing the policymap name command.
4.Link the class maps to the policy maps by issuing the classname command. 5.Define one or more actions that should be taken for that traffic class.
6.Link the policy map to an interface by issuing the servicepolicy {input | output} name command.

Bandwidth guarantees are set in policymap class configuration mode. You can specify the bandwidth as a rate or as a percentage with the bandwidth and priority commands. The syntax of the priority command is priority {bandwidth | percentpercentage} [burst], where bandwidth is specified in Kbps and burst is specified in bytes. The prioritycommand creates a strictpriority queue where packets are dequeued before packets from other queues are dequeued. The strictpriority queue is given priority over all other traffic.
If no priority traffic is being sent, the other traffic classes can share the remainingbandwidth based on their configured values.
The bandwidth command specifies a guaranteed amount of bandwidth for a particular traffic class. The syntax of the bandwidth command is bandwidth {kbps | remaining percentpercentage | percentpercentage}, where kbps is the amount of bandwidth that is guaranteed to a particular traffic class.
In this scenario, Voice over IP (VoIP) traffic is given a guaranteed 20 percent of the interface's bandwidth. Video traffic is given a guaranteed 40 percent of the interface's bandwidth. Voice and video traffic can exceed these bandwidth percentages if any unused bandwidth remains.
The remaining 40 percent, or 40 Mbps, of the interface's bandwidth can be used by other traffic. If traffic does not match any traffic class, it will become part of the classdefault class. In this scenario, web traffic belongs to the classdefault class. Therefore, web traffic can consume 25 percent of the remaining bandwidth. If no other traffic is being sent on the interface, web traffic can consume 25 percent of the interface's bandwidth. However, when voice and video traffic are heavy, web traffic can consume 25 percent of the remaining 40 Mbps, which is equal to 10 Mbps.
Even less web traffic can be sent if File Transfer Protocol (FTP)

traffic or other unclassifiedtraffic is heavy. FTP traffic can consume 50 percent of the remaining bandwidth on the interface. If no other traffic is being sent on the interface, FTP traffic can consume 50 percent of the interface's bandwidth. During periods of heavy voice and video usage, FTP traffic can consume 50 percent of the remaining 40 Mbps, which is equal to 20 Mbps.

Reference:
https://www.cisco.com/c/en/us/support/docs/quality-of-service-qos/qos-packet-marking/10100-priorityvsbw.html

QUESTION 29

On which of the following interfaces can a port ACL be applied? (Select 3 choices.)

A.   an SVI
B.   a trunk port
C.   an EtherChannel interface
D.   a routed port
E.   a Layer 2 port

Correct Answer: (Look at the end of the book)

Explanation/Reference:
Explanation:
A port access control list (PACL) can be applied to a trunk port, a Layer 2 port, or an EtherChannel interface. PACLs filter inbound Layer 2 traffic on a switch port interface; PACLs cannot filter outbound traffic. When PACLs are applied on a switch, packets are filtered based on several criteria, including IP addresses, port numbers, or upperlayer protocol information. If a PACL is applied to a trunk port, it will filter all virtual LAN (VLAN) traffic traversing the trunk, including voice and data VLAN traffic. A PACL can be used with an EtherChannel configuration, but the PACL must be applied to the logical EtherChannel interface? physical ports within the EtherChannel group cannot have a PACL applied to them. PACLs cannot be applied to a switch virtual interface (SVI) or to a

routed port. An SVI is a virtual interface that is used as a gateway on a multilayer switch. SVIs can be used to route traffic across Layer 3 interfaces. However, PACLs can only be applied to Layer 2 switching interfaces. Furthermore, because PACLs operate at Layer 2, they cannot be applied to routed ports, which operate at Layer 3.

Reference:
https://www.cisco.com/c/en/us/td/docs/switches/lan/catalyst650 0/ios/12-2SX/configuration/guide/book/vacl.html#wp1119764

QUESTION 30

Which of the following is true regarding the structure of a VPN ID? (Select the best answer.)

A.   It begins with a 4-byte VPN index and ends with a 6-byte MAC address.
B.   It begins with an 8-byte RD and ends with a 4-byte IPv4 address.
C.   It begins with a 4-byte IPv4 address and ends with a 3-byte OUI.
D.   It begins with a 3-byte OUI and ends with a 4-byte VPN index.
E.   It begins with a 6-byte MAC address and ends with a 4-byte IPv4 address.

Correct Answer: (Look at the end of the book)

Explanation/Reference:
Explanation:
A virtual private network (VPN) ID begins with a 3byte Organizationally Unique Identifier(OUI) and ends with a 4byte VPN index. The VPN ID identifies a VPN routing and forwarding (VRF). To update a VPN ID for a VRF, issue the vpn id oui: vpn-index command from VRF configuration mode.
Although a Media Access Control (MAC) address contains an OUI, a VPN ID does notcontain a MAC address. A VPN ID also does not contain a route distinguisher (RD) or an
IPv4 address. However, a multiprotocol Border Gateway Protocol

(BGP) VPNIPv4 address begins with an 8byte RD and ends with a 4byte IPv4 address.

Reference:
https://www.cisco.com/c/en/us/td/docs/ios/12_2/12_2b/12_2b4/feature/guide/12b_vpn.html

QUESTION 31

Which of the following statements are correct regarding NETCONF? (Select 2 choices.)

A.   NETCONF is an opensource cloudcomputing platform.
B.   NETCONF is a connectionless protocol.
• C.   NETCONF is a standardsbased protocol.
D.   NETCONF uses XML as the data modeling language.
∂ E.   NETCONF uses YANG as the data modeling language.

Correct Answer: (Look at the end of the book)

Explanation/Reference:
Explanation:
Network Configuration Protocol (NETCONF) is a standardsbased protocol that uses YANG as the data modeling language. NETCONF, which is described in Request for Comments (RFC) 6241, provides the ability to automate the configuration of network devices. YANG, which is defined in RFC 6020, is a hierarchical data modeling language that can model configuration and state data for NETCONF.
NETCONF does not use Extensible Markup Language (XML) as the data modeling language? NETCONF uses XML as its data encoding method. YANG data that is used by NETCONF is encoded in an XML format.
NETCONF is not a connectionless protocol. Rather, it is a connectionoriented protocol that requires a persistent, reliable connection. NETCONF connections must also provide confidentiality, integrity, authentication, and replay protection. Secure Shell (SSH) is the mandatory transport protocol for NETCONF.

NETCONF is not an opensource cloudcomputing platform. OpenStack is an opensource cloudcomputing platform. Each OpenStack modular component is responsible for a particular function, and each component has a code name. The following list contains several of the most popular OpenStack components:

-Nova -OpenStack Compute: manages pools of computer resources
-Neutron -OpenStack Networking: manages networking and addressing
-Cinder -OpenStack Block Storage: manages blocklevel storage devices
-Glance -OpenStack Image: manages disk and server images
-Swift -OpenStack Object Storage: manages redundant storage systems
-Keystone -OpenStack Identity: is responsible for authentication
-Horizon -OpenStack Dashboard: provides a graphical user interface (GUI)
-Ceilometer -OpenStackTelemetry: provides counterbased tracking that can be used for customer usage billing

Reference: https://tools.ietf.org/html/rfc6241
https://tools.ietf.org/html/rfc6020

QUESTION 32

Which of the following benefits is provided by fog computing? (Select the best answer.)

A.   It filters data before it goes to the cloud. ✎

B.   It ensures reliable connectivity to the cloud.
C.   It allows more data to be stored in the cloud.
D.   It allows data to be transmitted to the cloud faster.

Correct Answer: (Look at the end of the book)

Explanation/Reference:
Explanation:
Fo computing filters data before it goes to the cloud. Fog computing

is a method designed to alleviate the challenges of processing the data generated by Internet of Things (IoT) devices and transmitting that data to the cloud. IoT devices, which are often called embedded devices or smart objects, are typically lowpower, lowmemory devices with limited processing capabilities. These devices are used in a variety of applications, such as environmental monitoring, healthcare monitoring, process automation, and location tracking. Many embedded devices can transmit data wirelessly, and some are capable of transmitting over a wired connection. However, connectivity is generally unreliable and bandwidth is often constrained.

Io devices are numerous, and they produce a lot of data. For example, an airplanegenerates 10 terabytes (TB) of data for every 30 minutes of flight, and a tagged cow can generate an average of 200 megabytes (MB) of data per year. However, IoT devices often do not have the processing power to analyze the data, nor do they have the power or bandwidth to transmit a lot of data. Fog computing addresses these concerns by storing, processing, and filtering IoT data locally, sending only critical information to the cloud.

Fo computing does not ensure reliable connectivity to the cloud. However, because fogcomputing handles most of the data locally, security and resiliency of the data are increased.

Fo computing does not allow more data to be stored in the cloud. However, because fogcomputing processes and filters data before it is sent to the cloud, the cloud storage space can be filled with relevant data rather than irrelevant, unprocessed data.

Fo computing does not allow data to be transmitted to the cloud faster. However, because fog computing selectively chooses only the most relevant data to send to the cloud, more bandwidth is freed up for data to be sent.

Reference:
https://developer.cisco.com/site/iox/documents/developer-guide/?ref=fog

QUESTION 33

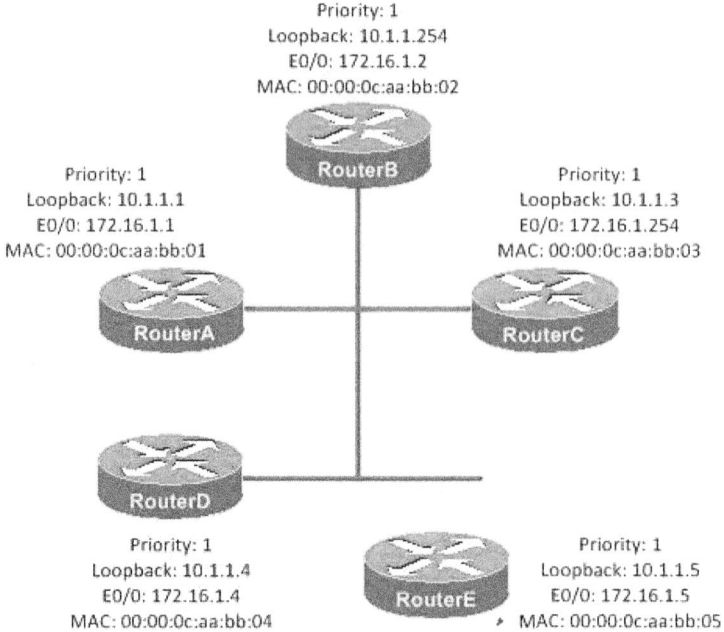

Priority: 1
Loopback: 10.1.1.254
E0/0: 172.16.1.2
MAC: 00:00:0c:aa:bb:02

Priority: 1
Loopback: 10.1.1.1
E0/0: 172.16.1.1
MAC: 00:00:0c:aa:bb:01

Priority: 1
Loopback: 10.1.1.3
E0/0: 172.16.1.254
MAC: 00:00:0c:aa:bb:03

Priority: 1
Loopback: 10.1.1.4
E0/0: 172.16.1.4
MAC: 00:00:0c:aa:bb:04

Priority: 1
Loopback: 10.1.1.5
E0/0: 172.16.1.5
MAC: 00:00:0c:aa:bb:05

You administer the IS-IS network shown in the exhibit above. A DIS has been elected on the multiaccess segment.
Which of the following routers will be the DIS after you connect RouterE to the multiaccess segment? (Select the best answer.)

A.   RouterA
B.   RouterB
C.   RouterC
D.   RouterD
E.   RouterE

Correct Answer: (Look at the end of the book)

Explanation/Reference:
Explanation:
RouterE will be the designated intermediate system (DIS) after you connect it to the multiaccess segment. The Intermediate SystemtoIntermediate System (IS-IS) DIS is analogous to the Open Shortest Path First (OSPF) designated router (DR). All ISIS routers

62

on the network segment establish adjacencies with the DIS. The DIS serves as a focal point for the distribution of ISIS routing information. If the DIS is no longer detected on the network, a new DIS is elected based on the priority of the remaining routers on the network segment.

The DIS for the multiaccess segment is the router with the highest interface priority. To configure the priority of an interface, you should issue the isis priority command from interface configuration mode. The syntax of the isis priority command is isis priorityvalue [level1 | level2], where value is an integer from 0 through 127. A router with an interface priority of 0 can still become the DIS. If you do not issue the isis prioritycommand on an interface, the default interface priority is 64. If interface priority values are equal, the router with the highest Media Access Control (MAC) address becomes the DIS if the multiaccess segment is a LAN. If the multiaccess segment is a Frame Relay link, the router with the highest datalink connection identifier (DLCI) becomes the DIS. If the DLCI is the same at both ends, the router with the higher system ID becomes the DIS. Every ISIS router is required to have a unique system ID. If two ISIS routers have the same system ID, an ISIS neighbor relationship will not form.

Unlike the DR in OSPF, the DIS in ISIS can be preempted if a router with a higher priority or a higher MAC address is connected to the network. In this scenario, all of the routers have the same interface priority. Therefore, the router with the highest MAC address becomes the DIS. Before RouterE is connected, RouterD is the DIS because it has the highest MAC address. However, after RouterE is connected, RouterE becomes the DIS because RouterE has a higher MAC address than RouterD.

Neither RouterA, RouterB, nor RouterC will become the DIS unless you increase the interface priority for that router's interface. Loopback addresses and interface IP addresses are not considered in the election of the DIS.

Reference:
https://www.cisco.com/c/en/us/products/index.html#wp38987

QUESTION 34

Which of the following statements is true about DiffServ class AF41? (Select the best answer.)

A.   AF41 has a low priority and a low drop probability.
B.   AF41 has a low priority and a high drop probability.
• C.   AF41 has a high priority and a low drop probability.
D.   AF41 has a high priority and a high drop probability.

Correct Answer: (Look at the end of the book)

Explanation/Reference:
Explanation:
DiffServ class AF41 has a high priority and a low drop probability. AF41 is a Differentiated Services Code Point (DSCP) value, which is a 6bit header value that identifies the Quality of Service (QoS) traffic class that is assigned to the packet. DSCP values beginning with AF are called Assured Forwarding (AF) perhop behaviors (PHBs), which are defined in Request for Comments (RFC) 2597. AF separates packets into four queue classes and three drop probabilities. The AF

values are specified in the format AFxy, where x is the queue class and y is the drop probability. The following table displays the AF values with their queue classes and drop rates:

Queue Class (x)	Low Drop (y = 1)			Medium Drop (y = 2)			High Drop (y = 3)		
	DSCP	Binary	Decimal	DSCP	Binary	Decimal	DSCP	Binary	Decimal
1	AF11	001010	10	AF12	001100	12	AF13	001110	14
2	AF21	010010	18	AF22	010100	20	AF23	010110	22
3	AF31	011010	26	AF32	011100	28	AF33	011110	30
4	AF41	100010	34	AF42	100100	36	AF43	100110	38

AF11 has a low priority and a low drop probability. AF13 has a low priority and a high drop probability. AF43 has a high priority and a high drop probability.
The first three DSCP bits correspond to the queue class, the fourth and fifth DSCP bits correspond to the drop probability, and the sixth bit is always set to 0. To quickly convert AF values to decimal values, you should use the formula $8x + 2y$. For example, AF41 converts to a decimal value of 34, because $(8 \times 4) + (2 \times 1) = 32 + 2 = 34$. Packets with higher AF values are not necessarily given preference over packets with lower AF values. Packets with a higher queue class

value are given queuing priority over packets with a lower queue class, but packets with a higher drop rate value are dropped more often than packets with a lower drop rate value.

Reference:
https://www.cisco.com/c/en/us/support/docs/quality-of-service-qos/qos-packet-marking/10103-dscpvalues.html#assured

QUESTION 35

Which of the following command sets correctly configures basic IPv6toIPv4 connectivity for NAT-PT? (Select the best answer.)

A.   Router(config)#ipv6 nat prefix 2000:ABC::/32
      Router(config)#ipv6 nat
B.   Router(config)#ipv6 nat prefix 2000:ABC::/64
      Router(config)#ipv6 nat
C.   Router(config)#ipv6 nat prefix 2000:ABC::/96
      Router(config)#ipv6 nat
D.   Router(config)#ipv6 nat prefix 2000:ABC::/32
      Router(config)#interface fastethernet 1/1
      Router(configif)#ipv6 nat
      Router(configif)#interface fastethernet 1/2
      Router(configif)#ipv6 nat
E.   Router(config)#ipv6 nat prefix 2000:ABC::/64
      Router(config)#interface fastethernet 1/1
      Router(configif)#ipv6 nat
      Router(configif)#interface fastethernet 1/2
      Router(configif)#ipv6 nat
F.   Router(config)#ipv6 nat prefix 2000:ABC::/96
      Router(config)#interface fastethernet 1/1
      Router(configif)#ipv6 nat
      Router(configif)#interface fastethernet ½
      Router(configif)#ipv6 nat

Correct Answer: (Look at the end of the book)

Explanation/Reference:
Explanation:
The following command set correctly configures basic IPv6toIPv4 connectivity for Network Address TranslationProtocol Translation (NATPT):

Router(config)#ipv6 nat prefix 2000:ABC::/96
Router(config)#interface fastethernet 1/1
Router(configif)#ipv6 nat
Router(configif)#interface fastethernet 1/2
Router(configif)#ipv6 nat

NAT-PT is used to enable communication between IPv4only hosts and IPv6only hosts by translating IPv4 packets to IPv6 packets and IPv6 packets to IPv4 packets. To enable NATPT, you must assign a global NATPT prefix, enable NATPT on the incoming and outgoing interfaces, and create IPv4toIPv6 and IPv6toIPv4 address mappings. To assign a global NATPT prefix, you should issue the ipv6 nat prefixipv6prefix/ prefixlength command from global configuration mode, where prefixlength is always 96. Therefore, the ipv6 nat prefix 2000:ABC::/32 command and the ipv6 nat prefix 2000:ABC::/64 command are invalid.

To enable NATPT on an interface, you should issue the ipv6 nat command from interface configuration mode on the incoming and outgoing interfaces. You cannot issue the ipv6 nat command from global configuration mode.

A NATPT router must contain IPv6toIPv4 and IPv4toIPv6 address mappings so that the router knows how to correctly translate IPv4 and IPv6 addresses. There are four methods for using NATPT:

-IPv4mapped NATPT
-Static NATPT
-Dynamic NATPT
-Port Address Translation (PAT)

IPv4mapped NATPT enables IPv6 traffic to be sent to an IPv4 network without requiring that IPv6 destination address mapping be configured. To configure IPv4mapped NATPT, you should issue the ipv6 nat prefix ipv6prefixv4mapped {accesslistname | ipv6prefix} command from global configuration mode or interface configuration mode.

Static NATPT creates static IPv6toIPv4 or IPv4toIPv6 address mappings. To create a static IPv6toIPv4 address mapping, you should issue the ipv6 nat v6v4 source ipv6address ipv4address command. To create a static IPv4toIPv6 mapping, you should issue the ipv6 nat v4v6 source ipv6address ipv4address command. Dynamic NATPT allocates IPv6toIPv4 or IPv4toIPv6 address mappings from a pool. When a session is established, a onetoone mapping is created? the mapping is then removed when the session is finished. To configure dynamic IPv6toIPv4 address mapping, you should issue the ipv6 nat v6v4 source {list accesslistname | routemapmapname} pool poolname command. You should then create the address pool by issuing the ipv6 nat v6v4 pool poolname startipv4 endipv4 prefixlength prefixlengthcommand. To configure dynamic IPv4toIPv6 address mapping, you should issue the ipv6 nat v4v6 sourcelist {accesslistnumber | accesslistname} pool poolname command. You should then create the address pool by issuing the ipv6 nat v4v6 pool poolname startipv6 endipv6 prefixlength prefixlength command.

PAT allows multiple IPv6 addresses to be mapped to one or more IPv4 addresses. To use PAT with a single IPv4 address, you should issue the ipv6 nat v6v4 source {list accesslistname | routemap mapname} interface interfacenameoverload command. To use PAT with a pool of IPv4 addresses, you should issue the ipv6

nat v6v4 source {listaccesslistname | routemap mapname} pool poolnameoverload command. You should then create the address pool by issuing the ipv6 nat v6v4 pool poolname startipv4 endipv4 prefixlength prefixlength command.

Reference:
https://www.cisco.com/c/en/us/td/docs/ios-xml/ios/ipv6/configuration/xe-3s/ipv6-xe-36s-book/ip6-nat-trnsln.html

QUESTION 36

In what order will a Rapid-PVST+ switch port pass through the port states? (Select the best answer.)

A.   blocking, spanning, listening, forwarding
* B.   discarding, learning, forwarding
C.   blocking, listening, learning, forwarding
D.   learning, discarding, forwarding

E.   blocking, learning, listening, forwarding

F.   Ports enter the forwarding state immediately

Correct Answer: (Look at the end of the book)

Explanation/Reference:

Explanation:

A Rapid-Per-VLAN Spanning Tree Plus (PVST+) switch port will pass through the following states:

-Discarding

-Learning

-Forwarding

RapidPVST combines the rapid transition of ports by Rapid Spanning Tree Protocol (RSTP) with the creation of spanning trees for each virtual LAN (VLAN) by PVST+. RSTP improves the slow transition of a Spanning Tree Protocol (STP) port to the forwarding state, thereby increasing convergence speed.

STP is used to eliminate loops in a switched network that is designed with redundant paths. There can be only one active path at any given time between any two endpoints on an Ethernet network. If multiple paths between the same two endpoints exist at the same time, switching loops can occur. STP activates and deactivates links dynamically to allow the network to respond to and reroute traffic around a failed link.

When RSTP is enabled, each port first enters the discarding state, in which a port receives bridge protocol data units (BPDUs) and directs them to the system module? however, the port neither sends BPDUs nor forwards any frames. The switch port then transitions to the learning state, in which it begins to transmit BPDUs and learn addressing information. Finally, a switch port transitions to the forwarding state, in which the switch port forwards frames. If a switch port determines at any time during the RSTP state process that a switching loop would be caused by entering the forwarding state, the switch port again enters the discarding state, in which the switch receives BPDUs and directs them to the system module but does not send BPDUs or forward frames.

STP port states are somewhat different from RSTP port states. A switch port will pass through the following STP states after a switch is turned on:

-Blocking
-Listening
-Learning
-Forwarding

When STP is enabled and a switch is turned on, each port first enters the blocking state, which is similar to the RSTP discarding state. The switch port then transitions to the listening state, in which it begins processing BPDUs as it listens for information to determine whether it should transition to the learning state. After entering the learning state, a switch port begins to transmit BPDUs and learn addressing information with which to build the switching database. Finally, a switch port transitions to the forwarding state, in which the switch port forwards frames. If a switch port determines at any time during the STP state process that a switching loop would be caused by entering the forwarding state, the switch port enters the disabled state, in which the switch receives BPDUs but does not direct them to the system module.

The primary differences between STP and RSTP are the port states and the speed of convergence. By default, STP takes 50 seconds to converge. By contrast, RSTP takes less than 10 seconds to converge. Switch ports do not immediately enter the forwarding state when the switch is first turned on, unless PortFast is enabled on the port. PortFast enables a switch port to go directly to the forwarding state rather than pass through the normal STP or RSTP states. However, you should enable PortFast only on switch ports that are connected directly to endpoint workstations? otherwise, switching loops may occur.

Blocking and listening are valid STP port states but are not valid RSTP port states. Spanning is not a valid STP or RSTP port state.

Reference:
https://www.cisco.com/c/en/us/support/docs/lan-switching/spanning-tree-protocol/24062-146.html
www.cisco.com/en/US/tech/tk389/tk621/technologies_tech_note09186a0080094797.shtml
https://www.cisco.com/c/en/us/support/docs/switches/catalyst-6500-series-switches/72836-rapidpvst-mig-config.html

QUESTION 37

Which of the following regular expression characters should be placed at the end of a BGP AS path filter to indicate the originating AS? (Select the best answer.)

- ○ A. $
- B.   ^
- C.   *
- D.   ]
- E.   .
- F.   _

Correct Answer: (Look at the end of the book)

Explanation/Reference:
Explanation:
The dollar sign ($) regular expression character should be placed at the end of a Border Gateway Protocol (BGP) autonomous system (AS) path filter to indicate the originating AS. Regular expressions are used to locate character strings that match a particular pattern. AS path filters are used to permit or deny routes that match the regular expression.

The $ character indicates that the preceding characters should match the end of the string. The originating router will insert its AS number into the AS path, and subsequent routers will prepend their AS numbers to the beginning of the AS path string. The last AS number in the AS path is the originating AS. For example, the ip as-path access-list 1 permit ^111_999$ command permits paths that originate from AS 999.

The caret (^) character should be placed at the beginning of a BGP AS path filter to indicate the AS from which the path was learned. The ^ character indicates that

the subsequent characters should match the start of the string. The first number in an AS path indicates the AS from which the path was learned. For example, the ip aspath accesslist 1 permit ^111_999$ command permits paths that are learned from AS 111.
The underscore (_) character is used to indicate a comma, a brace,

the start or end of an input string, or a space. When used between two AS path numbers, the _ character indicates that the ASes are directly connected. For example, the ip aspath accesslist 1 permit ^111_999$ command indicates that AS 111 and AS 999 should be directly connected.

The period (.) character is used to represent any single character. For example, the ip aspath accesslist 1 permit ^..._999$ command permits paths that originate from AS 999 and are learned from any threedigit AS.

The bracket ([]) character is used to indicate a set of characters or a range of characters. For example, the ip aspath accesslist 1 permit ^[09]_999$ command permits paths that originate from AS 999 and are learned from any AS numbered from 0 through 9, and the ip aspath accesslist 1 permit ^[123]_999$ command permits paths that originate from AS 999 and are learned from AS 1, AS 2, or AS 3.

The asterisk (*) character indicates zero or more sequences of the previous expression. For example, the expression [09]* indicates a string of zero or more digits. Therefore, the ip aspath accesslist 1 permit ^111_ [09]*$ command permits paths that are learned from AS 111 and originate from any AS.

Reference:
https://www.cisco.com/c/en/us/support/docs/ip/border-gateway-protocol-bgp/13754-26.html
https://www.cisco.com/c/en/us/td/docs/ios/12_2/termserv/confiiguration/guide/ftersv_c/tcfaapre.html
https://supportforums.cisco.com/t5/other-service-provider-subjects/bgp-regular-expression-as-path-filter/td-p/1821020

QUESTION 38

You issue the following commands on RouterB:

```
RouterB(config)#interface fa0/0
RouterB(config-if)#ip authentication mode eigrp 19 md5
RouterB(config-if)#ip authentication key-chain eigrp 19 ExSim
RouterB(config-if)#exit
RouterB(config)#key chain ExSim
RouterB(config-keychain)#key 1
RouterB(config-keychain-key)#key-string Boson
RouterB(config-keychain-key)#key 19
RouterB(config-keychain-key)#key-string ExSim
RouterB(config-keychain-key)#key 37
RouterB(config-keychain-key)#key-string NetSim
```

Which of the following key strings will RouterB use when sending EIGRP packets? (Select the best answer.)

A. Boson
B. ExSim
C. NetSim
D. any of the three key strings

Correct Answer: (Look at the end of the book)

Explanation/Reference:
Explanation:
RouterB will use the key string Boson when sending Enhanced Interior Gateway Routing Protocol (EIGRP) packets. EIGRP supports Message Digest 5 (MD5) authentication of routing updates to prevent a router from receiving routing updates from unauthorized routers. Authentication is configured on a perinterface basis. To configure an interface to authenticate EIGRP packets, you should first enter interface configuration mode by issuing the interfacetype number command from global configuration mode. Next, you should enable MD5 authentication by issuing the ip authentication mode eigrp autonomoussystemmd5 command in interface configuration mode. Finally, you should issue the ip authentication keychain eigrpautonomoussystem keychain command in interface configuration mode to specify the key chain that should be used. In this scenario, RouterB is configured for EIGRP autonomous system (AS) 19.
To create a key chain, you should issue the key chain chainname command from global configuration mode. The chain name is locally significant; it is used only to match a set of keys with a local router

interface. Therefore, key chain names do not have to match between neighbor routers. In this scenario, RouterB is configured with the key chain name ExSim.

After you create a key chain, you must specify at least one key number by issuing the keynumber command in keychain configuration mode, where number is an integer from 0 through 2147483647. If multiple key commands are used to create multiple keys, the numbers do not need to be sequential. When sending EIGRP packets, the router will use the lowestnumbered key. Therefore, RouterB will use key 1 when sending EIGRP packets. When receiving EIGRP packets, the router will use any valid key that is configured on the router. Therefore, RouterB can use any of the keys when receiving EIGRP packets. However, the key numbers must match on each router; if a neighbor router uses the key string NetSim, it must also be assigned key number 37.

Each key can have only one authentication string. To specify the authentication string, you should issue the keystring text command in keychain key configuration mode, where text is a string of up to 80 casesensitive letters and numbers; the first character cannot be a number.

Reference:
https://www.cisco.com/c/en/us/td/docs/ios-xml/ios/iproute_pi/command/iri-cr-book/iri-cr-a1.html#wp3605671872

QUESTION 39

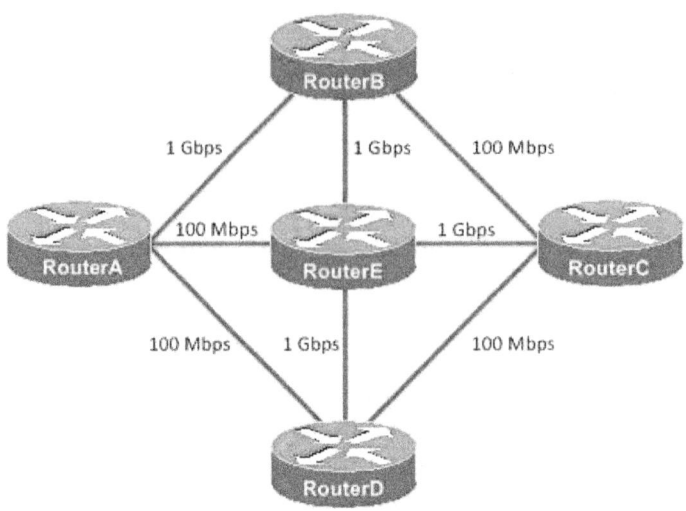

You administer the OSPF network shown in the diagram above. The reference bandwidth has been changed to 1000 on every router in the network. What is the cost of the route from RouterA to RouterC? (Select the best answer.)

A. 2
B. 3
C. 11
D. 12
E. 20

Correct Answer: (Look at the end of the book)

Explanation/Reference:
Explanation:
In this scenario, the cost of the route from RouterA to RouterC is 3. In an Open Shortest Path First (OSPF) network, a cost is associated with every link on the network. The OSPF routing process on each router calculates the optimal route to other routers in the network based on the sum of the link costs to those routers. The route with the lowest cost is considered the best. If there is more than one route with the same cost, then the OSPF routing process will use load balancing to

distribute traffic evenly among the routes. The cost of each link and the optimal route from RouterA to RouterC are shown in the following exhibit:

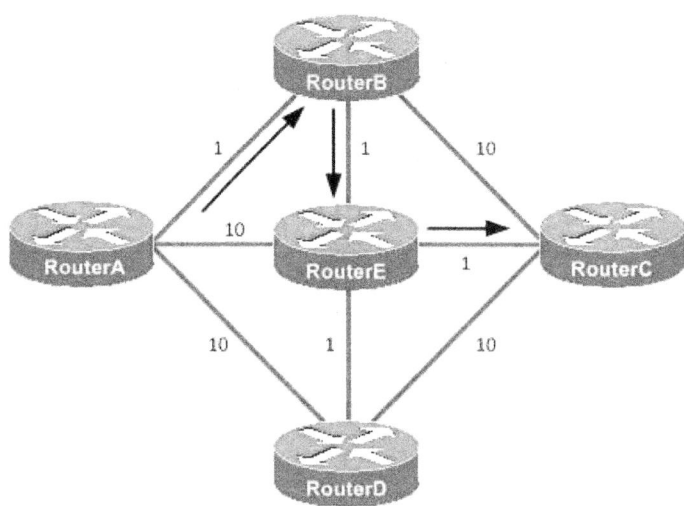

The cost of a link is based on the interface bandwidth and the reference bandwidth, as indicated by the following formula: cost = reference bandwidth / interface bandwidth

The default reference bandwidth is 100 Mbps. If a bandwidth has not been configured on an interface, the OSPF process will use the default value for the interface type. For example, a 100Mbps Fast Ethernet interface has a default interface bandwidth of 100. The minimum supported cost for an OSPF interface is 1, and any values that calculate to less than 1 are rounded up to 1. Therefore, any link with an interface bandwidth greater than or equal to 100 Mbps will result in a cost of 1 by default. In this scenario, the reference bandwidth is 1000 Mbps. Thus a FastEthernet interface will have a cost of 10, and a 1Gbps GigabitEthernet interface will have a cost of 1.

An OSPF process uses cost values to generate its shortest path first (SPF) tree and then to determine the optimal routes to all known networks. Because the minimum cost value is 1, the reference bandwidth should be a value greater than or equal to the bandwidth of the fastest routed link in the administrative domain. If the reference bandwidth is less than the fastest routed link on the network, a situation can arise where the costs of two interfaces are the same even though their link speeds are different. For example, if the reference bandwidth in this scenario were reset to its default value, the cost of every link would have a value of 1.

Because all links would then appear to have the same cost, the OSPF routing process would not be able to distinguish between the FastEthernet and GigabitEthernet links in the network. The OSPF process would then perform equalcost load balancing to distribute packets evenly among the available paths. This distribution would cause some packets in this example to take suboptimal routes to their destinations.

You can issue the autocost command from router configuration mode to change the reference bandwidth for an OSPF routing process. The syntax for the autocost command is autocost reference-bandwidth ref-bw, where ref-bw is an integer between 1 and 4294967. Alternatively, you can manually configure a cost at the interface level by issuing the ip ospf cost command.

Reference:
https://www.cisco.com/c/en/us/support/docs/ip/open-shortest-path-first-ospf/7039-1.html#t6

QUESTION 40

Which of the following information does a Type 2 LSA contain? (Select the best answer.)

A.   subnet information for an entire area
B.   external routes redistributed into OSPF
C.   the router ID and the IP addresses for a single router
D.   subnet and router information for all the routers on a segment

Correct Answer: (Look at the end of the book)

Explanation/Reference:
Explanation:

A Type 2 linkstate advertisement (LSA) contains subnet and router information for all the routers on a segment. Type 2 LSAs, which are also called network LSAs, are generated by only the designated router (DR) to each of the segments connected to the DR. These LSAs are not propagated outside the area in which they originate? they are flooded only within the local area.

A Type 1 LSA contains the router ID and the IP addresses for a single router. Type 1 LSAs, which are also called router LSAs, are generated by all Open Shortest Path First (OSPF) routers on a segment. Like Type 2 LSAs, Type 1 LSAs are not propagated outside the area in which they originate; they are flooded only within the local area.

A Type 3 LSA contains subnet information for an entire area. Type 3 LSAs, which are also called network summary LSAs, are generated by area border routers (ABRs). Unlike Type 1 and Type 2 LSAs, Type 3 LSAs are advertised between areas throughout an autonomous system (AS) except into totally stubby areas.

A Type 5 LSA contains external routes redistributed into OSPF. Type 5 LSAs, which are also called ASexternal LSAs, are generated by autonomous system boundary routers (ASBRs). Therefore, Type 5 LSAs are advertised throughout an AS except into stub areas, totally stubby areas, and notsostubby areas (NSSAs).

Reference:
https://www.cisco.com/c/en/us/td/docs/switches/datacenter/sw/4_2/nx-os/unicast/configuration/guide/l3_cli_nxos/l3_ospf.html#wp1243056
https://www.cisco.com/c/en/us/td/docs/security/fwsm/fwsm32/asdm52f/user/guide/asdmug/mon_rtg.html#wp1046958

QUESTION 41

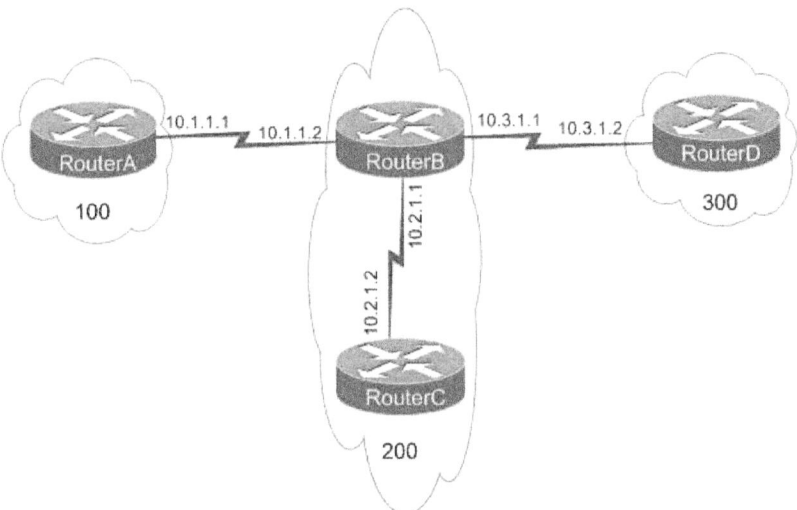

You administer the network shown above. You issue the show running-config command on RouterA and receive the following partial output:

```
router bgp 100
 network 192.168.0.0
 network 192.168.1.0
 neighbor 10.1.1.2 remote-as 200
 neighbor 10.1.1.2 send-community
 neighbor 10.1.1.2 route-map map1 out
 !
route-map map1 permit 10
 match ip address 1
 set community no-export
 !
route-map map1 permit 20
 !
access-list 1 permit 192.168.0.0 0.0.0.255
```

Which of the following statements are true? (Select 2 choices.)

A.   RouterA will not advertise any routes to RouterB.

B.   RouterA will advertise only the route to 192.168.1.0/24 to RouterB.

C.   RouterA will advertise the routes to 192.168.0.0/24 and 192.168.1.0/24 to RouterB.

D.   RouterB will not advertise any routes to RouterD.

E.   RouterB will advertise only the route to 192.168.0.0/24 to RouterD.

F.   RouterB will advertise only the route to 192.168.1.0/24 to RouterD.

G.   RouterB will advertise the routes to 192.168.0.0/24 and 192.168.1.0/24 to RouterD.

Correct Answer: (Look at the end of the book)

Explanation/Reference:
Explanation:
RouterA will advertise the routes to 192.168.0.0/24 and 192.168.1.0/24 to RouterB, and RouterB will advertise only the route to 192.168.1.0/24 to RouterD. RouterB will advertise both routes to RouterC because RouterB and RouterC are in the same autonomous system (AS). The neighbor 10.1.1.2 routemap map1 out command applies route map map1 to modify outgoing routes from RouterA. Because the routemap map1 permit 20 command overrides the implicit deny rule for map1, the route map will not restrict which routes are advertised from RouterA to RouterB. Additionally, map1 is configured to only apply the noexport community attribute to routes that match access list 1. Routes that do not match access list 1 are advertised without the attribute. Because route map map1 is configured to

apply the noexport community attribute to only the routes that pass access list 1, the noexport community attribute will affect only the route to 192.168.0.0/24. The neighbor 10.1.1.2 remoteas 200 command specifies that RouterB, which is in AS 200, is an external Border Gateway Protocol (eBGP) neighbor of RouterA. The neighbor 10.1.1.2 sendcommunity command configures RouterA to send community attribute settings to RouterB. The community attribute is an optional,
transitive Border Gateway Protocol (BGP) attribute that is not required to be supported by all BGP implementations. Additionally, BGP implementations that do not support the community attribute are not required to pass the attribute to other routers. By default, Cisco routers do not pass community attributes to BGP neighbors. The community attribute can be modified in a route map by issuing

the set community command with one of the following four keywords:

-no-advertise -prevents advertisements to any BGP peer
-no-export-prevents advertisements to eBGP peers
-loca-las -prevents advertising outside the AS, or in confederation scenarios, outside the sub-AS internet-advertises the route to any router

The set community no-export command configures the BGP community attribute to inform neighbor routers to not export the route to eBGP peers. Therefore, RouterB will not advertise the route to 192.168.0.0/24 outside of AS 200. Because RouterD is in AS 300, RouterB will not advertise the 192.168.0.0/24 route to RouterD. RouterB will advertise both routes to RouterC, which is in AS 200. The community attribute does not modify how RouterA advertises the routes; it modifies how neighbor routers advertise the routes received from RouterA.

Reference:
https://www.cisco.com/c/en/us/support/docs/ip/border-gateway-protocol-bgp/26634-bgp-toc.html#communityattribute
https://www.cisco.com/c/en/us/support/docs/ip/border-gateway-protocol-bgp/26634-bgp-toc.html#sec3
https://www.cisco.com/c/en/us/td/docs/ios-xml/ios/iproute_bgp/command/irg-cr-book/bgp-n1.html#wp2607806244

QUESTION 42

You are configuring 802.1X authentication on the FastEthernet 0/1 port on a switch named SwitchA. You want to ensure that any hosts connected to the port are authenticated by using 802.1X before the hosts can transmit data through the switch.
Which of the following command sequences should you issue on SwitchA? (Select the best answer.)

A. SwitchA#configure terminal
SwitchA(config)#aaa newmodel
SwitchA(config)#aaa authentication dot1x default group radius

SwitchA(config)#dot1x systemauthcontrol
SwitchA(config)#interface fastethernet 0/1
SwitchA(configif)#dot1x portcontrol forceauthorized

B. SwitchA#configure terminalSwitchA(config)#aaa newmodel
SwitchA(config)#aaa authentication dot1x default group radius
SwitchA(config)#dot1x systemauthcontrol
SwitchA(config)#interface fastethernet 0/1
SwitchA(configif)#dot1x portcontrol forceunauthorized

C. SwitchA#configure terminalSwitchA(config)#aaa newmodel
SwitchA(config)#aaa authentication dot1x default group radius
SwitchA(config)#dot1x systemauthcontrol
SwitchA(config)#interface fastethernet 0/1
SwitchA(configif)#dot1x portcontrol auto

D. SwitchA#configure terminal
SwitchA(config)#aaa newmodel
SwitchA(config)#aaa authentication dot1x default group radius
SwitchA(config)#dot1x systemauthcontrol
SwitchA(config)#interface fastethernet 0/1
SwitchA(configif)#dot1x portcontrol all

Correct Answer: (Look at the end of the book)
Section: (none)
Explanation

Explanation/Reference:
Explanation:
You should issue the following command sequence on SwitchA to
ensure that hosts connected to the FastEthernet 0/1 port are
authenticated by using 802.1X before the hosts are allowed to send
traffic through the switch:

SwitchA#configure terminal
SwitchA(config)#aaa newmodel
SwitchA(config)#aaa authentication dot1x default group radius
SwitchA(config)#dot1x systemauthcontrol
SwitchA(config)#interface fastethernet 0/1
SwitchA(configif)#dot1x portcontrol auto

You can enable 802.1X portbased authentication on Cisco switches to ensure that only authenticated users can send traffic through the switch. Before a user is authenticated, the only traffic allowed through the switch port is Extensible Authentication Protocol over LANs (EAPOL), Spanning Tree Protocol (STP), and Cisco Discovery Protocol (CDP) traffic. This ensures that the host is not able to send traffic through the port until authentication occurs.

To configure 802.1X authentication on a switch, you should first enable Authentication, Authorization, and Accounting (AAA) authentication on the switch by issuing the aaa newmodel command in global configuration mode. A Remote Authentication DialIn User Service (RADIUS) server must exist on the network in order to support AAA authentication. After configuring AAA authentication on the switch, you should issue the aaa authentication dot1x default group radius command to configure the switch to use the RADIUS servers for authentication.

You should enable 802.1X on the switch after you have configured AAA authentication on the switch. You can enable 802.1X by issuing the dot1x system authcontrol command. This command globally enables 802.1X on the switch. You should then configure each interface that will use 802.1X. In this scenario, you want to configure interface FastEthernet 0/1, so you should issue the interface fastethernet 0/1 command to enter interface configuration mode. After entering interface configuration mode, you should issue the dot1x portcontrol {forceauthorized | forceunauthorized | auto} command. The auto keyword enables 802.1X authentication on the port? consequently, the authentication process occurs between the switch and a connected host. If the host is configured with 802.1X authentication, the host will be authenticated and will be able to send traffic through the switch.

If the host is not configured with 802.1X authentication, the authentication process will fail and the host will be unable to send traffic through the port. The force authorized keyword of the dot1x portcontrol command configures the port to authorize any host that connects to the port? no 802.1X authentication process will take place. Any host connected to the port will be able to send traffic through the switch. The force unauthorized keyword configures the port to never allow authentication for a connected host. No authentication will take place, and the host will be unable to send traffic through the port.

The command sequence that contains the dot1x portcontrol all command does not configure 802.1X authentication on the FastEthernet 0/1 port on SwitchA. The dot1x portcontrol command does not include an all parameter. Issuing this command would result in an error being displayed.

Reference:
https://www.cisco.com/c/en/us/td/docs/switches/lan/catalyst375 0/software/release/12- 2_25_se/configuration/guide/3750scg/sw8021x.html#wp1025133

QUESTION 43

Two routers have been set up to establish a VPN tunnel. Both routers support GRE and IPSec, and both routers are configured with IPv4 and IPv6 addresses. You issue the tunnel mode auto command on both routers.
Which of the following statements is true? (Select the best answer.)

A.   GRE will be used for the tunneling protocol, and IPv4 will be used for the transport protocol.
B.   GRE will be used for the tunneling protocol, and IPv6 will be used for the transport protocol.
C.   IPSec will be used for the tunneling protocol, and IPv4 will be used for the transport protocol.
D.   IPSec will be used for the tunneling protocol, and IPv6 will be used for the transport protocol.
E.   The tunnel will not establish, because one router must be configured statically.

Correct Answer: (Look at the end of the book)

Explanation/Reference:
Explanation:
The tunnel will not establish, because one router, the initiator, must be configured statically. The tunnel mode auto command enables the Tunnel Mode Auto Selection feature, which simplifies the configuration of a virtual private network (VPN) tunnel. When Tunnel Mode Auto Selection is configured, the responder will apply

the tunneling protocol and transport protocol that is established by the initiator.

To configure a router to use Generic Routing Encapsulation (GRE) for the tunneling protocol and IPv4 for the transport protocol, you should issue the tunnel mode gre ipcommand. To configure a router to use GRE for the tunneling protocol and IPv6 for the transport protocol, you should issue the tunnel mode gre ipv6 command. To configure a router to use IP Security (IPSec) for the tunneling protocol and IPv4 for the transport protocol, you should issue the tunnel mode ipsec ipv4 command. To configure a router to use IPSec for the tunneling protocol and IPv6 for the transport protocol, you should issue the tunnel mode ipsec ipv6 command.

Reference:
https://www.cisco.com/c/en/us/td/docs/ios-xml/ios/sec_conn_vpnips/configuration/xe-3s/sec-sec-for-vpns-w-ipsec-xe-3s-book/sec-ipsec-virt-tunnl.html#concept_D55B0B7783A441BBB576E9F85693DF39
https://www.cisco.com/c/en/us/td/docs/ios-xml/ios/security/s1/sec-s1-cr-book/sec-cr-t2.html#wp3291311677

QUESTION 44

You issue the show ip route command on RouterE and receive the following output:

```
O    192.0.4.0/24 [110/2] via 10.1.1.13, 00:00:08, FastEthernet1/0
O    192.0.5.0/24 [110/65] via 10.1.1.17, 00:00:08, Serial0/0
C    192.0.6.0/24 is directly connected, FastEthernet2/0
     10.0.0.0/30 is subnetted, 4 subnets
O       10.1.1.8 [110/65] via 10.1.1.13, 00:00:08, FastEthernet1/0
C       10.1.1.12 is directly connected, FastEthernet1/0
O       10.1.1.0 [110/65] via 10.1.1.13, 00:00:08, FastEthernet1/0
C       10.1.1.16 is directly connected, Serial0/0
O    192.0.3.0/24 [110/66] via 10.1.1.13, 00:00:08, FastEthernet1/0
```

Which of the following statements are accurate about the route to 192.0.3.0/24? (Select 2 choices.)

A.   The link cost is 66.
B.   The link cost is 110.
gC.   The AD is 66.

84

D.   The AD is 110.
E.   The bandwidth of the link is 66 Kbps.
F.   The bandwidth of the link is 110 Kbps.

Correct Answer: (Look at the end of the book)

Explanation/Reference:
Explanation:
The administrative distance (AD) of the route in the scenario is 110, and the link cost is 66. In the output of the show ip route command, the first number within the brackets indicates the AD. When multiple routes to a network exist and each route uses a different routing protocol, a router prefers the routing protocol with the lowest AD. The following list contains the most commonly used ADs:

Route Source	Distance
Connected route	0
Static route	1
EIGRP summary route	5
eBGP	20
Internal EIGRP	90
IGRP	100
OSPF	110
IS-IS	115
RIP	120
External EIGRP	170
iBGP	200
Unknown	255

The AD of the route in this scenario is 110, the same as the default distance for an Open Shortest Path First (OSPF) route. AD for a routing protocol can be manually configured by issuing the distance command in router configuration mode. For example, to change the AD of OSPF process ID 1 from 110 to 80, you could issue the following commands:

RouterE(config)#router ospf 1
RouterE(config-router)#distance 80

The second number within the brackets indicates the metric. Because this is an OSPF link, as indicated by the O at the start of the route statement, the second number within the brackets indicates the cost metric. Therefore, the cost of the link in this scenario is 66. When two OSPF paths exist to the same destination, the router will choose the OSPF path with the lowest cost.

OSPF calculates cost based on the bandwidth of an interface: the higher the bandwidth, the lower the cost. To calculate the cost, divide 100,000,000 by the bandwidth in bits per second. Thus a 100Mbps link would have a cost of 1, a 10Mbps link would have a cost of 10, a T1 line would have a cost of 64 (100,000,000 / 1,544,000), and a 64Kbps line would have a cost of 1,562.

As the hops between a router and a destination increase, the cost increases by the bandwidth calculation of the additional links. Therefore, the route in this scenario is the cost of the FastEthernet link between RouterE and RouterC added to the cost of the T1 link between RouterC and RouterB added to the cost of the FastEthernet link between RouterB and the 192.0.3.0/24 network. Therefore, the cost for RouterE to reach the 192.0.3.0/24 network is 1 + 64 + 1, or 66.

Reference:
https://www.cisco.com/c/en/us/td/docs/ios/12_2/iproute/comm and/reference/fiprrp_r/1rfindp2.html#wp1022511

QUESTION 45

You have issued the following commands on RouterA:

Pseudowire-class boson ip pmtu

RouterA receives a packet that is larger than the path MTU and that has a DF bit set to 0. Which of the following will RouterA do? (Select 2 choices.)

A.   RouterA will forward the packet.
B.   RouterA will drop the packet.
C.   RouterA will return an ICMP unreachable message to the sender.
D.   RouterA will fragment the packet before L2TP/IP encapsulation occurs.

E.   RouterA will fragment the packet after L2TP/IP encapsulation has occurred.

Correct Answer: (Look at the end of the book)

Explanation/Reference:
Explanation:
When RouterA receives a packet that is larger than the path maximum transmission unit (MTU) and that has a Don't Fragment (DF) bit set to 0, RouterA will fragment the packet before Layer 2 Tunneling Protocol (L2TP)/IP encapsulation has occurred and then forward the packet. The ip pmtu command enables path MTU discovery (PMTUD) so that fragmentation issues can be avoided on the service provider backbone.
With PMTUD, the DF bit is copied from the IP header to the Layer 2 encapsulation header. If an IP packet is larger than the MTU of any interface on the path, the packet is dropped or fragmented based on the DF bit. If the DF bit is set to 0, the packet is fragmented before encapsulation occurs and is then forwarded. If the DF bit is set to 1, the packet is dropped and the router will return an Internet Control Message Protocol (ICMP) unreachable message to the sender.

Reference:
https://www.cisco.com/c/en/us/td/docs/ios/12_0s/feature/guide/l2tpv30s.html#wp1065029
https://www.cisco.com/c/en/us/td/docs/ios/12_0s/feature/guide/l2tpv30s.html#wp1065029

QUESTION 46

In which of the following locations does BGP PIC store an alternate path? (Select the best answer.)

A.   only in the RIB
B.   only in the FIB
C.   only in CEF
D.   only in the RIB and the FIB
E.   in the RIB, in the FIB, and in CEF

Correct Answer: (Look at the end of the book)

Explanation/Reference:
Explanation:
Border Gateway Protocol (BGP) Prefix-Independent Convergence (PIC) improves convergence by creating and storing an alternate path in the Routing Information Base (RIB), in the Forwarding Information Base (FIB), and in Cisco Express Forwarding (CEF). As soon as a failure is detected, BGP uses the alternate path.
BGP PIC is capable of improving convergence for both core and edge failures on IPv4, IPv6, and Multiprotocol Label Switching (MPLS) networks. Bidirectional Forwarding Detection (BFD) must be enabled on directly connected neighbors in order to detect link failures.

Reference:
https://www.cisco.com/c/en/us/td/docs/routers/7600/ios/15S/c
onfiguration/guide/7600_15_0s_book/BGP.html

QUESTION 47

Which of the following can be monitored by the EEM IOSWDSysMon core event publisher? (Select the best answer.)

A.   abnormal stop events
B.   memory utilization
C.   syslog messages
D.   timed events
E.   counter thresholds

Correct Answer: (Look at the end of the book)

Explanation/Reference:
Explanation:
Memory utilization can be monitored by the Embedded Event Monitor (EEM) Watchdog System Monitor (IOSWDSysMon) core

event publisher. Watchdog System Monitor can also be configured to monitor CPU utilization.

EEM consists of three components: the EEM server, event publishers, and event subscribers. EEM event detectors are event publishers; EEM policies are event subscribers. When an event is detected, EEM can perform various actions, such as generating a Simple Network Management Protocol (SNMP) trap or reloading the router.

Abnormal stop events are monitored by the system manager event detector. Syslog messages are monitored by the syslog event detector. Timed events are monitored by the timer event detector. Counter thresholds are monitored by the counter event detector. All of these event detectors are considered to be EEM core event publishers.

Reference:
https://search.cisco.com/search?query=Cisco%20IOS%20Network%20Management%20Configuration%20Guide&locale=enUS&tab=Cisco

QUESTION 48

Which of the following are characteristics of GLBP? (Select 2 choices.)

A.   One router is elected as the active router, and another router is elected as the standby router.
B.   One router is elected as the master router, and all other routers are placed in the backup state.
C.   All routers in a GLBP group can participate by forwarding a portion of the traffic.
D.   In a GLBP group, only one AVG and only one AVF can be assigned.
E.   In a GLBP group, only one AVG can be assigned but multiple AVFs can be assigned.F. In a GLBP group, multiple AVGs can be assigned but only one AVF can be assigned.

Correct Answer: (Look at the end of the book)

Explanation/Reference:

Explanation:

The following are characteristics of Gateway Load Balancing Protocol (GLBP):

-All routers in a GLBP group can participate by forwarding a portion of the traffic.

-Only one active virtual gateway (AVG) can be assigned in a GLBP group, but multiple active virtualforwarders (AVFs) can be assigned in a GLBP group.

GLBP is a Ciscoproprietary protocol used to provide router redundancy and load balancing. GLBP enables you to configure multiple routers into a GLBP group; the routers in the group receive traffic sent to a virtual IP address that is configured for the group. Each GLBP group contains an AVG that is elected based on which router is configured with the highest priority value or the highest IP address value if multiple routers are configured with the highest priority value.

The other routers in the GLBP group are configured as primary or secondary AVFs. The AVG assigns a virtual Media Access Control (MAC) address to up to four primary AVFs; all other routers in the group are considered secondary AVFs and are placed in the listen state. The virtual MAC address is always 0007.b400.xxyy, where xx is the GLBP group number and yy is the AVF number.

When the AVG receives Address Resolution Protocol (ARP) requests that are sent to the virtual IP address for the GLBP group, the AVG responds with different virtual MAC addresses. This provides load balancing, because each of the primary AVFs will participate by forwarding a portion of the traffic sent to the virtual IP address. If one of the AVFs fails, the AVG assigns the AVF role to another router in the group. If the AVG fails, the AVF with the highest priority becomes the AVG; by default, preemption is disabled.

Additionally, you can control the percentage of traffic that is sent to a specific gateway by configuring weighted load balancing. By default GLBP uses a roundrobin technique to load balance between routers. If you configure weighted load balancing, GLBP can send a higher percentage of traffic to a single GLBP group member based on the weight values assigned to the interfaces of that member.

The election of an active router and a standby router are

characteristics of Hot Standby Router Protocol (HSRP), not GLBP. Like GLBP, HSRP provides router redundancy. However, only one router in an HSRP group is active at any time. If the active router becomes unavailable, the standby router becomes the active

router.
The election of a master router and the placement of all other routers in the group into the backup state are characteristics of Virtual Router Redundancy Protocol (VRRP). Like GLBP and HSRP, VRRP provides router redundancy. However, similar to HSRP, only one router is active at any time. If the master router becomes unavailable, one of the backup routers becomes the master router.
A GLBP group can contain only one AVG. All other routers in the group are configured as AVFs; multiple AVFs can be configured in a GLBP group.

Reference:
https://www.cisco.com/c/en/us/td/docs/ios/12_2s/feature/guide /fs_glbp2.html#wp1024997

QUESTION 49

Which of the following DSCP values has a binary value of 101110? (Select the best answer.)

A.   AF11
B.   AF23
C.   AF42
D.   CS1
E.   CS5
F.   EF

Correct Answer: (Look at the end of the book)

Explanation/Reference:
Explanation:
The Differentiated Services Code Point (DSCP) value EF has a binary value of 101110, which is equal to a decimal value of 46. DSCP values are sixbit header values that identify the Quality of

Service (QoS) traffic class that is assigned to the packet. The Expedited Forwarding (EF) per-hop behavior (PHB), which is defined in Request for Comments (RFC) 2598, indicates a high-priority packet that should be given queuing priority over other packets but should not be allowed to completely monopolize the interface. Voice over IP (VoIP) traffic is often assigned a DSCP value of EF.

DSCP values beginning with CS are called Class Selector (CS) PHBs, which are defined in RFC 2475. CS values are backward compatible with three-bit IP precedence values; the first three bits of the DSCP value correspond to the IP precedence value, and the last three bits of the DSCP value are set to 0. Packets with higher CS values are given queuing priority over packets with lower CS values. The following table displays the CS values with their binary values, decimal values, and IP precedence category names:

DSCP Value	Binary	Decimal	IP Precedence
CS0	000000	0	Routine
CS1	001000	8	Priority
CS2	010000	16	Immediate
CS3	011000	24	Flash
CS4	100000	32	Flash Override
CS5	101000	40	Critical
CS6	110000	48	Internetwork Control
CS7	111000	56	Network Control

DSCP values beginning with AF are called Assured Forwarding (AF) PHBs, which are defined in RFC 2597. AF separates packets into four queue classes and three drop priorities. The AF values are specified in the format AFxy, where x is the queue class and y is the drop priority. The following table displays the AF values with their queue classes and drop rates:

Queue Class (x)	Low Drop (y = 1)			Medium Drop (y = 2)			High Drop (y = 3)		
	DSCP	Binary	Decimal	DSCP	Binary	Decimal	DSCP	Binary	Decimal
1	AF11	001010	10	AF12	001100	12	AF13	001110	14
2	AF21	010010	18	AF22	010100	20	AF23	010110	22
3	AF31	011010	26	AF32	011100	28	AF33	011110	30
4	AF41	100010	34	AF42	100100	36	AF43	100110	38

The first three DSCP bits correspond to the queue class, the fourth and fifth DSCP bits correspond to the drop priority, and the sixth bit is always set to 0. To quickly convert AF values to decimal values, you should use the formula $8x + 2y$. For example, AF42 converts to a decimal value of 36, because $(8 \times 4) + (2 \times 2) = 32 + 4 = 36$. Packets with higher AF values are not necessarily given preference over packets with lower AF values. Packets with a higher queue class value are given queuing priority over packets with a lower queue class, but packets with a higher drop rate value are dropped more often than packets with a lower drop rate value.

Reference:
https://www.cisco.com/c/en/us/support/docs/quality-of-service-qos/qos-packet-marking/10103-dscpvalues.html#expeditedforwarding

QUESTION 50

Which of the following OSPFv3 LSA types is an intraareaprefix LSA? (Select the best answer.)

A.   Type 3

B.   Type 4
C.   Type 5
D.   Type 8
E.   Type 9

Correct Answer: (Look at the end of the book)

Explanation/Reference:
Explanation:
Open Shortest Path First version 3 (OSPFv3) Type 9 linkstate advertisements (LSAs) are intraareaprefix LSAs. OSPFv3 Type 9 LSAs carry IPv6 prefix information, much like OSPF version 2 (OSPFv2) Type 1 and Type 2 LSAs carry IPv4 prefix information. In OSPFv3, Type 1 and Type 2 LSAs no longer carry route prefixes. LSAs carry only routing information; they do not contain a full

network topology. Both Type 9 LSAs and Type 8 LSAs are new in OSPFv3.

OSPFv3 Type 8 LSAs are link LSAs. Type 8 LSAs are used to advertise the router's linklocal IPv6 address, prefix, and option information. These LSAs are never flooded outside the local link.

OSPFv3 Type 3 LSAs are interareaprefix LSAs for area border routers (ABRs). Type 3 LSAs are used to advertise internal networks to other areas. Like Type 9 LSAs, Type 3 LSAs also carry IPv6 prefix information.

OSPFv3 Type 4 LSAs are interarearouter LSAs for autonomous system boundary routers (ASBRs). Type 4 LSAs are used to advertise the location of an ASBR so that routers can determine the best nexthop path to an external network.

OSPFv3 Type 5 LSAs are autonomous system (AS)external LSAs. Type 5 LSAs are used to advertise external routes that are redistributed into OSPF.

Reference:
https://search.cisco.com/search?query=Cisco%20IOS%20IPv6%20 Configuration%20Guide&locale=enUS&tab=Cisco

QUESTION 51

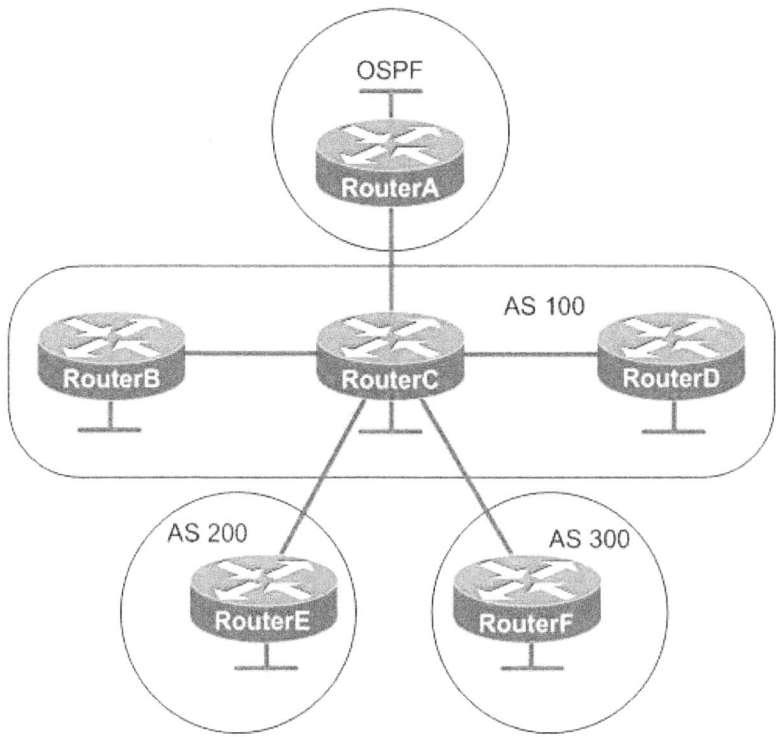

You administer the networks shown above. RouterA is connected to network A, RouterB is connected to network B, and so on. RouterB and RouterD are iBGP peers of RouterC; RouterE and RouterF are eBGP peers of RouterC. RouterA and RouterC are OSPF neighbors. RouterC, which is not configured as a route reflector, receives routes from all of the other routers on the network. You have issued the network command on each router to advertise their respective networks. You have also issued the redistribute command on RouterC to redistribute the OSPF routes from RouterA into BGP. Routes to which of the following networks will RouterC advertise to RouterF? (Select the best answer.)

A.   only network C
B.   only networks B, C, and D
C.   only networks A, B, C, and D

D.   only networks A, B, C, D, and E
E.   networks A, B, C, D, E, and F

Correct Answer: (Look at the end of the book)

Explanation/Reference:
Explanation:
RouterC will advertise only networks A, B, C, D, and E to RouterF.
RouterC and RouterF are external Border Gateway Protocol (eBGP)
peers, which are BGP routers that belong to different autonomous
systems (ASes). An eBGP peer advertises the following routes to
another eBGP peer:

-Routes learned through internal BGP (iBGP)
-Routes learned through eBGP
-Routes learned through redistribution
-Routes originated by a network statement

The only route that RouterC will not advertise to RouterF is network
F, because RouterC originally learned of the route from RouterF.
When RouterF advertises network F to RouterC, RouterF adds the
AS number (ASN) to the AS_PATH. Routes with an AS_PATH that
contains the ASN of a BGP peer are not advertised back to that peer.

If RouterF were in AS 100, RouterF and RouterC would be iBGP
peers. The BGP split horizon rule states that routes learned through
iBGP are not advertised to iBGP peers. Therefore, an iBGP peer
advertises the following routes to another iBGP peer:

-Routes learned through eBGP
-Routes learned through redistribution
-Routes originated by a network statement

Because iBGP routes are not advertised to iBGP peers, one of the
following actions must be taken to enable routers running iBGP to
communicate:

-Configure a full mesh.
-Configure a confederation.
-Configure a route reflector.

A full mesh configuration enables each router to learn each iBGP route independently without passing through a neighbor. However, a full mesh configuration requires the most administrative effort to configure. A confederation enables an AS to be divided into discrete units, each of which acts like a separate AS. Within each confederation, the routers must be fully meshed unless a route reflector is established. A route reflector can be used to pass iBGP routes between iBGP routers, eliminating the need for a full mesh configuration. However, it is important to note that route reflectors advertise best paths only to route reflector clients. Additionally, if multiple paths exist, a route reflector will always advertise the exit point that is closest to the route reflector.

Reference:
CCIE Routing and Switching v5.0 Certification Guide, Volume 2, Chapter 1, Injecting Routes/Prefixes into the BGP Table, pp. 18-40

QUESTION 52

You are connecting host computers to a switch with 10/100/1000Mbps Gigabit Ethernet ports. All of the ports are configured to autonegotiate speed and duplex settings.

Which of the following will cause a mismatch condition? (Select the best answer.)

A.   connecting a NIC that is configured for halfduplex, 100Mbps operation
B.   connecting a NIC that is configured for fullduplex, 100Mbps operation
C.   connecting a NIC that is configured for fullduplex, 1000Mbps operation
D.   connecting a NIC that is configured to autonegotiate duplex and speed settings

Correct Answer: (Look at the end of the book)

Explanation/Reference:

Explanation:

Connecting a network interface card (NIC) that is configured for fullduplex, 100Mbps operation will cause a mismatch condition because the duplex modes on the NIC and on the port will be different. A NIC that has been manually configured to use fullduplex or halfduplex mode does not respond to a port that is attempting to autonegotiate duplex settings. When the autonegotiating port receives no reply, it will use the default duplex settings for that speed. If the port detects that it should transmit at 10 Mbps or 100 Mbps, the port will default to halfduplex mode? if the port detects that it should transmit at 1000 Mbps, the port will default to fullduplex mode.

You can detect a duplex mismatch by monitoring a switch for %CDP-4-DUPLEXMISMATCH error messages. Additionally, you can issue the show interfacesinterface command, which displays counter information. If you see an abnormal increase in frame check sequence (FCS) errors and alignment errors on a halfduplex port, you should suspect a duplex mismatch. An abnormal increase in FCS errors and runts on a fullduplex port is also an indicator of a duplex mismatch.

Connecting a NIC that is configured for halfduplex, 100Mbps operation will not cause a mismatch condition.

The port will detect that it should transmit at 100 Mbps; therefore, it will default to halfduplex mode. Configuring both switch ports for halfduplex mode would enable only one port to send data at a time; however, communication could still occur, albeit slowly.

Connecting a NIC that is configured for fullduplex, 1000Mbps operation will not cause a mismatch condition. The port will detect that it should transmit at 1000 Mbps; therefore, it will default to fullduplex mode.

Connecting a NIC that is configured to autonegotiate duplex and speed settings will not cause a mismatch condition. When both sides of a link autonegotiate speed settings, they will select the highest speed common to both of them. When both sides of a link autonegotiate duplex settings, they will negotiate fullduplex mode if both ports support fullduplex operation. If either side of the link does not support fullduplex operation, the ports will negotiate halfduplex mode.

Reference:

https://www.cisco.com/c/en/us/support/docs/switches/catalyst-6500-series-switches/17053-46.html#auto_neg_valid
https://www.cisco.com/c/en/us/support/docs/switches/catalyst-6500-series-switches/17053-46.html#ustand

QUESTION 53

Which of the following CHAP packets contains a Code field that is set to a value of 4? (Select the best answer.)

A.   Challenge
B.   Failure
C.   Response
D.   Success

Correct Answer: (Look at the end of the book)

Explanation/Reference:
Explanation:
A Challenge Handshake Authentication Protocol (CHAP) Failure packet contains a Code field that is set to a value of 4. A CHAP packet consists of the following fields:
-A oneoctet Code field
-A oneoctet Identifier field, which helps to match challenges to responses
-A twooctet Length field,which indicates the length of the packet
-One or more fields that are determined by the Code field

A Challenge packet has a Code field that is set to a value of 1. It also has the following additional fields:
-A oneoctet ValueSize field, which indicates the length of the Value field
-A variablelength ChallengeValue field, which contains a variable, unique stream of octets
-A variablelength Name field, which identifies the name of the transmitting device

A Response packet has a Code field that is set to a value of 2. It also has the following additional fields:

-A oneoctet ValueSize field, which indicates the length of the Response Value field
-A variablelength Response Value field, which contains a concatenated oneway hash of the ID, the secret key, and the Challenge Value
-A variablelength Name field, which identifies the name of the transmitting device
A Success packet has a Code field that is set to a value of 3. In addition to the standard fields, the Success packet and the Failure packet have a variablelength Message field, which displays a success or failure message, typically in humanreadable ASCII characters.

Reference:
https://www.cisco.com/c/en/us/support/docs/wan/point-to-point-protocol-ppp/25647-understanding-ppp-chap.html
https://www.ietf.org/rfc/rfc1994.txt

QUESTION 54

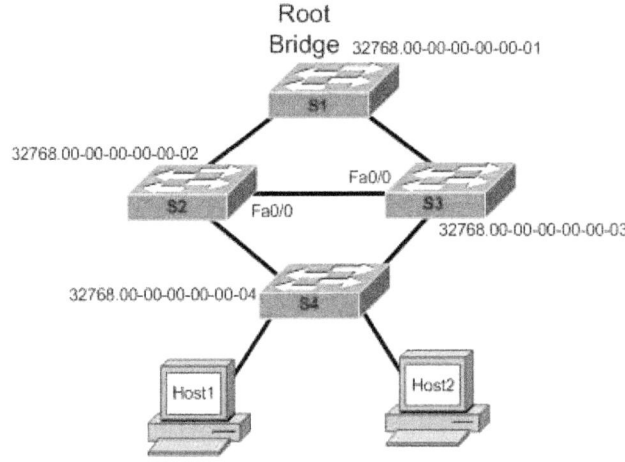

You administer the network shown in the exhibit above. You enable root guard by issuing the spanning-tree guard root command in interface configuration mode for the Fa0/0 interfaces of S2 and S3. Which of the following statements best describes what will occur if the link between S1 and S2 is broken? (Select the best answer.)

A.   Traffic will follow its normal path from Host2 to S1.

B.   The Fa0/0 port on both switches will be put into the root-inconsistent state.

C.   Only Fa0/0 on S2 will be put into the root-inconsistent state.

D.   Only Fa0/0 on S3 will be put into the root-inconsistent state.

E.   STP will be disabled.

Correct Answer: (Look at the end of the book)

Explanation/Reference:

Explanation:

If the link between S1 and S2 is broken, the Fa0/0 port on S2 will be placed into the root-inconsistent state. Root guard is typically used to prevent a designated port from becoming a root port, thereby influencing which bridge will become the root bridge on the network. When root guard is applied to a port, the port is permanently configured as a designated port. Normally, a port that receives a superior bridge protocol data unit (BPDU) will become the root port. However, if a port configured with root guard receives a superior BPDU, the port transitions to the rootinconsistent state and no data will flow through that port until it stops receiving superior BPDUs. As a result, root guard can be used to influence the placement of the root bridge on a network by preventing other switches from propagating

superior BPDUs throughout the network and becoming the root bridge.

When the root bridge detects the broken link, it will send out BPDUs to reconverge the network topology. Since root guard was enabled on Fa0/0 on S2, the interface will be placed into the rootinconsistent state when it receives superior BPDUs from Fa0/0 on S3. Thus root guard prevents Fa0/0 on S2 from being selected as a root port. The port will remain in the rootinconsistent state until it stops receiving superior BPDUs from Fa0/0 on S3.

Fa0/0 on S3 will not be placed into the rootinconsistent state, because it will not receive superior BPDUs from S2. S3 will continue to receive superior BPDUs from S1.

Traffic would not follow its normal path from Host2 to the root bridge if the link between S1 and S2 were broken. When the link between S1 and S2 is up, traffic from Host2 travels from S4 to S2 to S1. This is based on the root path cost. The root path cost is an accumulation of path costs from bridge to bridge. A Fast Ethernet link has a path cost of 19. There are two 100Mbps paths, so the root path cost from S4 to S2 to S1 equals 38. The root path cost from S4 to S3 to S1 also equals 38. If the root path cost is identical, the bridge ID is used to determine the path. In this scenario, S2 has a priority of 32768, as does S3. However, the Media Access Control (MAC) address for S2, 000000000002, is lower than the MAC address for S3, 000000000003, making S2 the designated bridge. If the link between S1 and S2 breaks, the path for traffic coming from Host2 will be rerouted from its normal path to the S4 to S3 to S1 path.

Spanning Tree Protocol (STP) would not be disabled if the link between S1 and S2 were to break. It is STP that reconverges the network topology to reroute traffic after a link in the root path becomes disabled.

Reference:
https://www.cisco.com/c/en/us/support/docs/lan-switching/spanning-tree-protocol/10588-74.html

QUESTION 55

Which of the following statements is true regarding Cisco IOS EPC? (Select the best answer.)

A.   Each capture point can be associated with multiple capture buffers.
B.   Multiple capture points can be active on a single interface.
C.   The buffer type and sampling interval are the only settings you can adjust when creating a capture buffer.
D.   The packet data contains a timestamp indicating when the packet was added to the buffer.

Correct Answer: (Look at the end of the book)

Explanation/Reference:
Explanation:

Multiple capture points can be active on a single interface. Cisco IOS Embedded Packet Capture (EPC) is a feature that you can implement to assist with tracing packets and troubleshooting issues with packet flow in and out of Cisco devices. To implement Cisco IOS EPC, you must perform the following steps:

1.Create a capture buffer. 2.Create a capture point. 3.Associate the capture point with the capture buffer. 4.Enable the capture point.

The buffer type and sampling interval are not the only settings you can adjust when creating a capture buffer; you can also adjust several other items, including the

buffer size and the packet capture rate. Specifying the sampling interval and the buffer type will allow for the maximum number of pertinent packets to be stored in the buffer. To configure a capture buffer, you should issue the monitor capture bufferbuffername [clear | exportexportlocation | filteraccesslistipaccesslist | limit {allownthpaknthpacket | duration seconds | packetcounttotalpackets | packetspersec packets} | [maxsize elementsize] [sizebuffersize] [circular | linear]] command from global configuration mode. The capture buffer contains packet data and metadata. The packet data does not contain a timestamp indicating when the packet was added to the buffer; the timestamp is contained within the metadata. In addition, the metadata contains information regarding the direction of transmission of the packet, the switch path, and the encapsulation type.

To create a capture point, you should issue the monitor capture point {ip | ipv6} {cefcapturepointname interfacename interfacetype {both | in | out} | processswitched capturepointname {both | fromus | in | out}} command from global configuration mode. You can create multiple capture points with unique names and parameters on a single interface.

To associate a capture point with a capture buffer, you should issue the monitor capture point associatecapturepointname capturebuffername command from global configuration mode. Each capture point can be associated with only one capture buffer. Finally, to enable the capture point so that it can begin to capture packet

data, you should issue the monitor capture point start
{capturepointname | all} command.

Reference:
https://www.cisco.com/c/en/us/td/docs/ios-
xml/ios/epc/configuration/15-mt/epc-15-mt-book/nm-packet-
capture.html#GUID-1A08B87D-D022-4F41-A0CB-
B30938EB9EF8

QUESTION 56

Which of the following connects more than two UNIs and enables
each UNI to communicate with every other UNI in the
configuration? (Select the best answer.)

A.   E-LAN
B.   EPL
C.   E-Tree
D.   EVPL

Correct Answer: (Look at the end of the book)

Explanation/Reference:
Explanation:
An ELAN service connects more than two User Network Interfaces
(UNIs) and enables each UNI to communicate with every other UNI
in the configuration. An ELAN is a multipointtomultipoint Ethernet
virtual connection (EVC). A UNI is the physical demarcation
between a service provider and a subscriber. ELAN services fully
mesh two or more UNIs and follow a specific set of rules for
delivering service frames to a UNI. Each UNI in an ELAN can
communicate with any other UNI in the ELAN. ELANs typically
have a distance limitation of 50 miles (80 kilometers). Layer 2 Virtual
Private Networks (L2VPNs) and multipoint L2VPNs are examples of
ELANs.
Both Ethernet private line (EPL) and Ethernet virtual private line
(EVPL) are Eline services. Eline services are Ethernet pointtopoint
EVC services that can be used to connect two UNIs. Therefore, an

Eline does not connect more than two UNIs. The difference between an EPL and an EVPL is that an EVPL is capable of service multiplexing. In addition, an EPL requires full service frame transparency. An EVPL does not.

An ETree is a pointtomultipoint EVC that resembles a hubandspoke configuration. Therefore, an ETree does not enable each UNI to communicate with every other UNI in the configuration. An ETree service connects more than one UNI to a single root UNI or leaf UNI. Root UNIs can send data to any leaf UNI. However, a leaf UNI can send traffic only to a root UNI. ETrees are typically used to provide Internet access to multiple sites.

Reference:
https://www.cisco.com/c/en/us/td/docs/net_mgmt/active_networ
k_abstraction/3-
7/service_activation/user/guide/anansaug/tech_overview.html#wp
1106296

QUESTION 57

Which of the following potential BGP enhancements were documented in the BGP Add-Paths proposal? (Select the best answer.)

A.   possible modifications to the best-path algorithm
B.   possible software upgrades for PE routers
C.   possible addition of a session between a route reflector and its client
D.   possible addition of a four-octet Path Identifier

Correct Answer: (Look at the end of the book)

Explanation/Reference:
Explanation:
The BGP Add-Paths proposal proposed the possible addition of a four-octet Path Identifier to Network Layer Reachability Information (NLRI) in order to enable Border Gateway Protocol (BGP) to distribute multiple paths. BGP as it is typically deployed has no

mechanism for distributing paths that are not considered the best path between speakers.

Observations about the possible addition of a session between a router reflector and its client were documented in Request for Comments (RFC) 6774, which discusses the distribution of diverse BGP paths. Specifically, RFC 6774 observed that BGP as it is typically deployed has no mechanism for distributing paths that are not considered the best path between speakers. However, the possible addition of a session between a route reflector and its client could enable a BGP router to distribute alternate paths.

Neither the AddPaths proposal nor RFC 6774 document possible modifications to the bestpath algorithm or software upgrades for provider edge (PE) routers. Although RFC 6774 does discuss a possible means of distributing paths other than the best path, the means by which BGP determines the best path to a destination were not changed. Therefore, no software upgrade is required.

Reference: https://tools.ietf.org/html/rfc6774

QUESTION 58

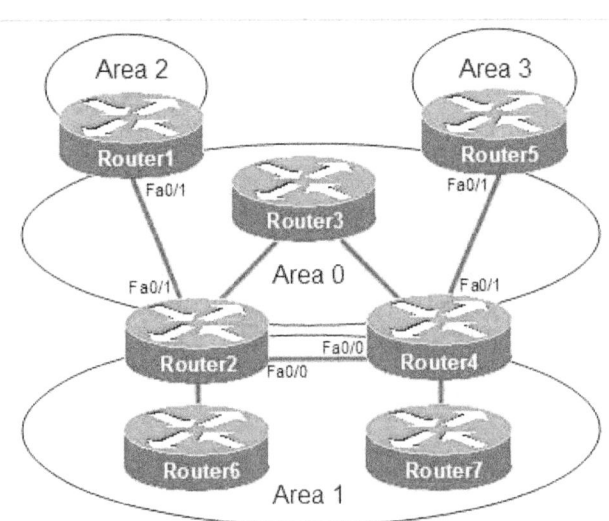

You administer the OSPF network shown in the diagram. Area 1 is configured as a standard area. Area 2 and Area 3 are configured as stub areas. Router3 fails. Several routes are lost throughout the

network.
Which of the following actions can you take to restore the lost
routes? (Select 2 choices.)

A.   Configure Area 1 as a stub area.
B.   Configure Area 2 and Area 3 as standard areas.
C.   Create a virtual link between Router1 and Router5.
D.   Create a virtual link between Router2 and Router4.
E.   Configure the Fa0/0 interfaces on Router2 and Router4 to be
part of Area 0.
F.   Configure the Fa0/1 interfaces on Router2 and Router4 with
IP addresses that were configured onRouter3.

Correct Answer: (Look at the end of the book)

Explanation/Reference:
Explanation:

You can take either of the following actions to restore the lost routes:
-       Create a virtual link between Router2 and Router4.
-       Configure the Fa0/0 interfaces on Router2 and Router4 to be
part of Area 0.

In this scenario, the backbone area, Area 0, has become
discontinuous, or partitioned, as shown in the following network
diagram:

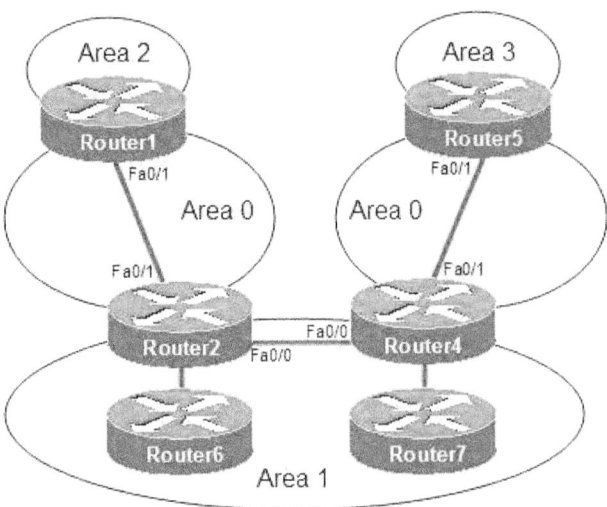

To connect a backbone area that has become discontinuous because of the loss of a router or the loss of a link between two routers, you can create a virtual link. The routers at each end of the virtual link must adhere to the following restrictions:

- Both routers must connect to the backbone area.
- Both routers must share another common area, which is used as a transit area.
- The transit area cannot be a stub area.
- The transit area cannot be the backbone area.

To create a virtual link, you should issue the area area-id virtual-link router-id command in router configuration mode on the routers at each end of the virtual link, where area-id is the transit area ID and routerid is the router ID of the router at the other end of the virtual link. For example, if the router ID of Router4 were 1.2.3.4, you would issue the area 1 virtual-link 1.2.3.4 command on Router2. You would also issue a similar command on Router4 by using the router ID of Router2 as the router-id parameter.
Alternatively, you can configure the Fa0/0 interfaces on Router2 and Router4 to be part of Area 0. Doing so would make Area 1 discontinuous. This is acceptable

because interarea traffic must pass through the backbone or a transit area; therefore, nonbackbone areas can be discontinuous. The discontinuous Area 1 partitions would be advertised to one another through inter-area routes instead of intra-area routes.

Configuring Area 1 as a stub area will not restore the lost routes. Additionally, configuring Area 1 as a stub area eliminates the possibility of using a virtual link to connect the discontinuous backbone areas.

Configuring Area 2 and Area 3 as standard areas will not restore the lost routes. Changing a stub area to a standard area will only allow Type 5 external summary routes to be advertised throughout the area. You cannot create a virtual link between Router1 and Router5. For a virtual link to be created, both routers must share a common area. If Router1 and Router5 shared a nonstub area, you could create a virtual link between them and the lost routes would be restored.

Configuring the Fa0/1 interfaces on Router2 and Router4 with IP addresses that were configured on Router3 will not restore the lost routes. The routes were not lost because of the unavailability of the IP addresses on Router3; the routes were lost because of the discontinuous backbone area.

Reference:
https://www.cisco.com/c/en/us/support/docs/ip/open-shortest-path-first-ospf/7039-1.html#t14
https://www.cisco.com/c/en/us/support/docs/ip/open-shortest-path-first-ospf/7039-1.html#t17

QUESTION 59

Which of the following ICMPv6 message types is sent by an IPv6capable host at startup? (Select the best answer.)

A.   router solicitation
B.   router advertisement
C.   neighbor solicitation
D.   neighbor advertisement

Correct Answer: (Look at the end of the book)

Explanation/Reference:

Explanation:

An Internet Control Message Protocol version 6 (ICMPv6) router solicitation message is sent by an IPv6capable host at startup. When IPv6 is enabled on a router interface, a linklocal address is created. Before the address is assigned to the interface, duplicate address detection (DAD) is performed to determine whether the IPv6 address is unique on the link. If DAD determines that the address is unique, the linklocal address is assigned to the interface and the router solicitation message is sent to the allrouters multicast address FF02::2. Hosts use router solicitation messages to request an immediate router advertisement.

A router advertisement that is sent in response to a router solicitation message is sent directly to the host that sent the router solicitation. Routers also send unsolicited router advertisements periodically to the allnodes multicast address FF02::1. Router advertisements contain the following information:

- The IPv6 address of the router interface attached to the link
- One or more IPv6 prefixes for the local link
- The lifetime for each prefix
- Flags that specify whether stateless or stateful autoconfiguration can be used
- The hop limit and maximum transmission unit (MTU) that the host should use

- Whether the router is a default router
- The amount of time that the router can be used as a default router

When a host receives a router advertisement, the IPv6 link-local prefix is added to the host's interface identifier to create the host's full IPv6 address. The first three octets of the interface identifier are set to the Organizationally Unique Identifier (OUI) of the Media Access Control (MAC) address of the interface. The fourth and fifth octets are set to FFFE. The sixth, seventh, and eighth octets are equal to the last three octets of the MAC address.

A host will send a neighbor solicitation message to determine the link-layer address of another host on the local link. Neighbor solicitation messages are sent with the sender's own link-layer address to the solicited-node multicast address. The solicited-node multicast address is created by adding the FF02::1:FF00/104 prefix to the last 24 bits of the destination host's IPv6 address. After a destination host's link-layer address is discovered, neighbor solicitations can be used to verify the reachability of a destination host.

When a host receives a neighbor solicitation message, it will reply with a neighbor advertisement message that contains the link-layer address of the host. The neighbor advertisement is sent directly to the host that sent the neighbor solicitation. A host will send an unsolicited neighbor advertisement whenever its address changes. Unsolicited neighbor advertisements are sent to the allnodes link-local multicast address FF02::1.

Reference:
Cisco: Implementing IPv6 Addressing and Basic Connectivity: IPv6 Router Advertisement Message IETF: RFC 4861: Neighbor Discovery for IP version 6 (IPv6)

QUESTION 60

Which of the following is true regarding RTC? (Select the best answer.)

A.   RTC sends only the prefixes that the PE router wants.
B.   RTC finds route inconsistencies.
C.   RTC synchronizes peers without a hard reset.
D.   RTC works with only VPNv4.
E.   RTC makes the ABR an RR and sets the next hop to self.

Correct Answer: (Look at the end of the book)

Explanation/Reference:
Explanation:
Route Target Constraint (RTC) sends only the prefixes that the Provider Edge (PE) router wants. In a normal Multiprotocol Label Switching (MPLS) virtual private network (VPN), the route reflector (RR) sends all of its VPN version 4 (VPNv4) and VPNv6 prefixes to the PE router. The PE router then drops the prefixes for which it does not have a matching VPN routing and forwarding (VRF). RTC

allows a PE router to send its route target (RT) membership data to the RR within an address family named rtfilter. The RR then uses rtfilter to determine which prefixes to send to the PE. In order for RTC to work, both the RR and the PE need to support RTC.

RTC does not find route inconsistencies, nor does it synchronize peers without a hard reset. This functionality is provided by Border Gateway Protocol (BGP) Enhanced Route Refresh.

BG Enhanced Route Refresh is enabled by default. If two BGP peers support EnhancedRoute Refresh, each peer will send a RouteRefresh StartofRIB (SOR) message and a RouteRefresh EndofRIB (EOR) message before and after an AdjRIBOut message, respectively. After a peer receives an EOR message, or after

the EOR timer expires, the peer will check to see whether it has any routes that were not readvertised. If any stale routes remain, they are deleted and the route inconsistency is logged.

RTC does not make the area border router (ABR) an RR, nor does it set the next hop to self. This behavior is exhibited by Unified MPLS. Unified MPLS increases scalability for an MPLS network by extending the label switched path (LSP) from end to end, not by redistributing interior gateway protocols (IGPs) into one another, but by distributing some of the IGP prefixes into BGP. BGP then distributes those prefixes throughout the network.

Reference:
https://www.cisco.com/c/en/us/support/docs/multiprotocol-label-switching-mpls/mpls/116062-technologies-technote-restraint-00.html
https://search.cisco.com/search?query=Cisco%20IOS%20BGP%20Configuration%20Guide&locale=enUS&tab=Cisco
https://www.cisco.com/c/en/us/support/docs/multiprotocol-label-switching-mpls/mpls/116127-configure-technology-00.html

Correct Answers

Question	Correct Answers
1	B
2	A
3	B
4	A
5	B
6	C
7	A
8	D
9	C
10	C
11	BD
12	A
13	D
14	A
15	E
16	C
17	BCE
18	D
19	BEG
20	A
21	D
22	D
23	B
24	B
25	E
26	CE
27	AE
28	A
29	BCE
30	D
31	CE

32	A
33	E
34	C
35	F
36	B
37	A
38	A
39	B
40	D
41	CF
42	C
43	E
44	AD
45	AD
46	E
47	B
48	CE
49	F
50	E
51	D
52	B
53	B
54	C
55	B
56	A
57	D
58	DE
59	A
60	A

Good Luck
in your exam!

By

Exam Boost

Printed in Great Britain
by Amazon